Debby,

Blessings & favor

from d. Howard

D1175028

ADVANCE PRAISE FOR
A JOURNEY BY FAITH:
NO RISK, NO REWARD

"Most people never live their dreams as entrepreneurs because they give up. Afraid of the risk. By reading Tina and Harold Lewis's book *A Journey by Faith*, those who are searching for what makes a successful business can discover the two most vital things: God and Family."

—ROLAND MARTIN, Journalist, TV commentator, TV One, CNN

"Everyone loves a love story. Here it is. A perfect love between Tina and Harold and their super successful entrepreneurial achievements, against all odds. It's beautiful, heart-touching, and profoundly inspiring. I predict you will like it."

—MARK VICTOR HANSEN, Co-creator of *Chicken Soup for the Soul* series

"Harold and Tina know the meaning of Success from the ground up. They understand the Value of hard work, drive and dedication. They just don't talk about it they live it. A remarkable story and remarkable couple!"

—STEDMAN GRAHAM, Author, Speaker

A JOURNEY
BY FAITH

NO RISK, NO REWARD

HAROLD AND TINA LEWIS

SAVIO
REPVBLIC

A SAVIO REPUBLIC BOOK
An Imprint of Post Hill Press

ISBN: 978-1-64293-122-8
ISBN (eBook): 978-1-64293-123-5

A Journey by Faith:
No Risk, No Reward
© 2019 by Harold and Tina Lewis
All Rights Reserved

Cover photo by LaMonte McLemore
Cover design by Tricia Principe, principedesign.com
Interior design and composition by Greg Johnson/Textbook Perfect

All Bible passages are quoted from the King James Version of the Bible.

posthillpress.com
New York • Nashville

Published in the United States of America

DEDICATION

We dedicate this book to our parents, Harold Lewis and Betty Lewis-Golder, and Charles and Mary-Ann Ricard. It's true that you can't pick your parents, but we couldn't have been more blessed with ours. Our journey would have never been possible without their love, support, encouragement, and vision. The postwar era brought many Black families to the West. As described in Isabel Wilkerson's book *The Warmth of Other Suns*, our parents were part of a great journey and migration. The journey that Tina and I have taken over the last forty-four years has been neither straight nor smooth, but through it all there have been far more good days than bad. We have been blessed and highly favored both spiritually and materially. We have been given more than we needed, and everything we wanted. There is a saying, "Beside every great man is a great woman." To my Tina I say, "In front of every great woman stands a well-directed man." We have been blessed with three wonderful children—Jeremy, and our twins, Jonathan and Jennifer—along with two wonderful grandchildren, Noah and Roman. We have lived by the maxim "From whom much has been given, much is expected." We hope that our legacy will bear this out and will be an inspiration to our children and others. Our hope is that at the end of our journey, we will have fulfilled our purpose in life, and we will hear the words of the Almighty, "Well done, my good and faithful servants." Through it all, we count it all good.

CONTENTS

PART THREE

FOREWORD

Presenting Tina and Harold's book is especially rewarding for me, and there are several reasons for that. On a personal level, getting to know Tina and Harold through the Trumpet Awards Foundation was, of course, very gratifying. They're simply good people, and it's great to spend time with them. I'm glad that their personalities come through on these pages.

I also saw how Harold and Tina embodied some qualities that I believe are powerful facilitators of success—and I mean success in the broadest and best sense of the word. While those attributes are certainly beneficial for anyone, they're especially relevant to African Americans, and are grounded in the African American experience going back many years.

I consider the faith-based foundation of Tina and Harold's life together to be the most important of these qualities. Faith of this kind includes formal religious observance, but it has larger meaning as well. It's the belief, or even the certainty, that we are here for a purpose. That purpose is to trust in God and to set an example of that trust for our children and everyone around us.

The vital importance of this kind of trust is demonstrated again and again in both the Old and New Testaments, and it can even be one of the key teachings of the Scriptures. In Exodus 14, Moses prays for God's help on the banks of the Red Sea. God answers, "Why do you cry out to me? Tell the people to go forward." And in Matthew 14, Jesus rebukes Peter: "O thou of little faith, wherefore didst thou doubt?" We should trust that we have the power to survive and overcome any obstacle, and we must act accordingly.

Harold and Tina's book is aptly titled *A Journey by Faith*, as it revisits the essence of trust in a modern context. This includes everything from corporate politics to raising children to facing dire health challenges.

While the goal of Tina and Harold's life is success, I want to emphasize again that this means success in a broad definition. It doesn't mean getting rich. In fact, I don't believe the word "rich" occurs even once in the book. From the beginning, everything Tina and Harold have undertaken was for creating a legacy for their children—as they themselves were given a legacy from their own parents of integrity, hard work, and unwavering faith.

Readers of this book will meet what I truly believe are two exemplary individuals, and an exemplary married couple as well. It's been a pleasure to know them, and I'm proud to introduce their book.

—Hon. Ambassador Andrew Young

INTRODUCTION

Delight yourself in the LORD,
and he will give you the desires of your heart.

—PSALM 37:4

It was one of those uniquely pleasant Southern California mornings that vacationers would love to take home with them. It was already special for me when just before noon I stepped out of my home on Mallard Court. Today I was going to fill the empty stall in my four-car garage with a dream.

Next door, my neighbor Jim groomed the grass beside his driveway. Jim, a perpetual gardener and handyman, looked up and we exchanged greetings. Then I waited for the truck to turn onto the cul-de-sac. The delivery was scheduled for noon.

A few minutes earlier the driver had called. He said, "Mr. Lewis, I have your car."

This was in 1999, the end of the twentieth century. The Soviet menace had expired. The dot-com boom and a generally strong economy was driving the stock market average past twelve thousand. California real estate was about to go through the roof.

It wouldn't last, of course, but this was a moment in history when the American dream seemed on course to realize its full potential.

Never had wealth been created at such a rate. Never had the number of millionaires increased so quickly and in such an unprecedented amount. A whole new class of wealthy people was arriving in Silicon Valley. If you weren't a billionaire yet, what were you waiting for?

Risk-takers and entrepreneurs were seeing opportunity all over the country, and especially in California. Money was abundant, and the money begat more money. Homes that once sold at affordable rates in middle-class neighborhoods were selling for a million dollars in cash, and "flipping houses" became the smart investor's road to riches.

Still, there were those whose faith remained in traditional, principled beliefs. They saw opportunity not in fast-buck enterprises, but in hard work, sacrifice, and perhaps even in divine intervention. I was one of these people, and today I felt that I had really arrived. My home was worth one million five hundred thousand dollars, and I owned several McDonald's restaurants in the San Diego area. Even if I wasn't a billionaire, I was doing well. I was grateful for this good fortune, and I was also proud that I had earned it.

Within big dreams are smaller ones. For decades one of my smaller dream had been to own a Ferrari. I'd owned some nice cars, but the Ferrari always sang to me, beckoned to me, promised itself to me, and now the Ferrari was on its way.

I heard the truck grinding along at a low speed as it turned the corner down the street. Yes, that truck was carrying a dark blue Ferrari 345 GT with a light blue interior, a two-hundred-miles-per-hour head turner for sure. It wasn't new, but it was pristine and *like* new.

I wore a big smile as the truck moved slowly up the street and came to a stop. The driver seemed to be checking the address. He glanced at me, then pulled the truck forward to the next house where Jim, bent over, was dealing with unruly weeds.

"Mr. Lewis," the driver called. "I'm here with your car."

Jim stood up and pointed toward me. "That's Mr. Lewis," he said.

As life had taught me, I patiently nodded. I knew what the driver saw: the extreme unlikelihood, or even the impossibility, that an African American man would own a Ferrari. I understood the perceptions, the presumptions, and the bias that dictated them. It wasn't racism, in my opinion, because there was no racist intention. There was just an assumption that had become a reflex over time. There was an assumption that the address for the delivery must be wrong, and the car must be going to the White man down the street.

But there was a something else too. Because I had encountered it so often, it was something I had wondered about. Maybe the mistaken assumption was not merely that an African American person would not be wealthy enough to own a high-priced car. After all, there were lots of conspicuously wealthy African Americans. Instead, perhaps the assumption was that an African American man would not own a high-priced car *unless he was an athlete or an entertainer.*

If I had been an NBA all-star or a Hall of Fame ballplayer, the driver would not have thought twice about my owning a Ferrari. I was convinced that two things were active in the driver's mind. First, here was a Black man. Second, here was a Black man who was not a celebrity. This noncelebrity Black man would not own a Ferrari.

Jim, however, was a different story. Since Jim was White, all things were possible. Jim might own a dozen Ferraris. Why not? It didn't matter that Jim wasn't an athlete. What mattered was that he was White.

There was a more important point, and it was one that I had come to understand over the course of my life. While many non-Black people shared the truck driver's assumptions about restricted sources of African American wealth, those same assumptions were accepted by many Black people, especially young Black people.

I had seen this often: African American boys whose hopes and dreams focused on the NBA or the NFL, or on Hollywood or the music industry. For almost all those boys, the aspirations were extremely unrealistic. The result was not only a waste of young people's time and energy, but often it was a waste of their real potential in other areas. Sometimes it was a genuinely tragic waste of their lives.

An important objective of this book is to widen the perspective on African American success. I was fortunate early in life to see celebrities up close. I want to share some of those experiences and what I learned from them. I want to show why I distanced myself not only from the longstanding racist depictions of subservient Blacks, but also from the newer clichés of what a successful Black person is supposed to be and do.

When I came into contact with stereotyped ideas about who I was and what I accomplished, I could feel some irritation. But I knew that showing anger was ultimately self-defeating. But keeping angry feelings bottled up could wear you down over time. There was no easy answer. You could either deal with the effects of all this or you couldn't. And if you couldn't, blaming someone else would not make the situation any better.

My ability to deal with those moments was largely responsible not just for how I became the owner of a Ferrari, but also how I became an entrepreneurial business owner, and the husband of an intelligent and accomplished woman, and the father of two sons and a daughter. It took hard work, sacrifice, belief, some timely decisions, a lot of risk, and a "hand up" (not a "hand out") that had been offered here and there.

I accepted the key to the Ferrari that day, and the unintended slight that came with it, the way I had accepted many such twists and turns.

I knew there would be more to come.

I also knew that many, many had come before.

My mother's father had been a wallpaper hanger. Her mother was a homemaker. All her life, church and family were the source of her strength. As a grown woman, church conventions were the highlight of the year. They were an opportunity to worship and to fellowship with friends from across the country.

It was at a convention in Pittsburgh that my mother stayed with Sister Eula McLaney and her two daughters, LaDoris and Bernice. It was common for church members in a hosting city to have people stay in their homes, as people had stayed in our home when conventions were in Los Angeles. Sister McLaney and her daughters loved to tell stories about watching my mother and my aunts descend the stairs going to church, wearing the gorgeous hats that were a tradition in the Black church. Since the days of slavery, Sunday was a chance to dress up and celebrate.

Throughout the years that my mother and Sister McLaney had become friends, my mother encouraged Sister McLaney to move from Pittsburgh to Los Angeles. Eventually this did happen. Sister McLaney arrived to find her calling and fortune.

In addition to working in the family business, my mother was a real estate broker. Sister McLaney wanted to open an assisted-living facility with her daughters. In Los Angeles, she found the perfect place, a small motel located on La Brea and Washington called the Flagstone Motel. It was owned by a White man, and when my mother showed the property, Sister McLaney made an offer to buy it.

My mother looked White, with hazel eyes. She was not trying to pass for White and, as a matter of fact, she got extremely angry when people thought she was White. In this case it worked to her advantage. When she took the offer to the owner of the motel, thinking she was White, he told her that he would not sell to any niggers.

Without reacting, my mother told him she understood. She followed that with her own offer, which the owner welcomed and accepted.

When she returned to Sister McLaney, she conveyed the owner's response and told her that she would purchase the property and upon closing would quick claim the property over to her. With that Sister McLaney gave my mother the money for the down payment and they were able to start a new life in Los Angeles.

Sister McLaney would, over the next years, become a millionaire owning assisted-living facilities and amassing a real estate portfolio to be envied. One of the first large purchases she made was to buy an estate in Holmby Hills, an extremely exclusive area of Los Angeles. It was a house that backed up to the home of Neil Diamond.

One day Sister McLaney and her daughters returned home and found the front door slightly ajar. Not knowing if they had left it open or if someone might be inside, they called the police.

In a few minutes the Beverly Hills police arrived and checked the house while Sister McLaney and her daughters waited outside. When the police returned, they told the ladies that everything was okay. Then an officer turned to them and said, "You ladies sure keep an immaculate house."

From Pittsburgh to Los Angeles and now living in Holmby Hills, they were still assumed to be housekeepers.

However, that isn't the end of the story. Sister McLaney did, in fact, find her fortune in Los Angeles, with the Flagstone Motel property as the start of it. Moreover, her daughter LaDoris has become a major philanthropist across the country and was even honored by the Los Angeles city council with a "LaDoris McLaney Day."

Of course, none of that would ever have happened if my mother or Sister McLaney had reacted to the intentional or unintentional disrespect that was directed at them. Sister McLaney wrote about this in her autobiography, *God, I Listened.*

I've tried to remember their example at moments like the car delivery, and there have been many of those moments. Tina, my wife, and I have had the hope that our children, like Sister McLaney's, would have a legacy that they could use to do good in the world.

Turning that hope into reality has been the purpose of our life and work together. This book is our story.

PART ONE

CHAPTER 1

Relentless Focus

*Do not conform to the pattern of this world but be
transformed by the renewing of your mind. Then you
will be able to test and approve what god's will is—his
good, pleasing and perfect will.*

—ROMANS 12:2

*If you don't design your own life plan, chances are
you'll fall into someone else's plan. And guess what
they have planned for you? Not much.*

—JIM ROHM

I was born in Baton Rouge, Louisiana, the eldest child of Charles
and Mary-Ann Ricard. I grew up with three younger brothers and
a younger sister. My family lived in a house next door to my grandmother's house. My father had built both the houses with his own
hands when he was nineteen years old.

This was the Deep South of segregation. Today that's seen as
a period of brutal racist oppression, which it was. But when I was
a child, it just seemed like a natural way of life, the way things
always were.

Tina

The first motor vehicle my father bought was a green Chevrolet pickup truck. Climbing into the back of the truck and going to the Dairy Queen were the longest trips I took except for the occasional visits to family in Mississippi. If we wanted something to eat on the way, we would stop for some sandwiches brought from home. There really wasn't any question of going to a restaurant in an unfamiliar town. It wasn't only a racial issue. It was also just being strangers. That could make people nervous in small Southern towns.

A very useful and important document for Black travelers in those days was *The Green Book.* This was a guide book that covered the entire United States, showing various locations and services that would be welcoming—and safe—for Black motorists. I'm not certain if my father used *The Green Book*. But knowing where to stop and where not to stop must have certainly been on his mind.

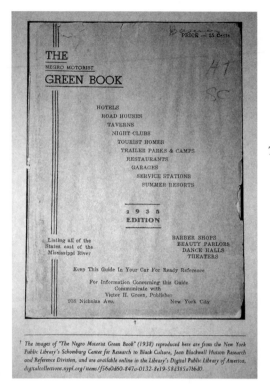

The Green Book

This page from *The Green Book* indicates some restaurants, barber shops, and gas stations in Louisiana that were open to Black travelers. "Tourist homes" refers to private residences in which a room could be rented for the night. Staying in segregated hotels or motels was simply not going to happen, and even inquiring about that could be a big mistake.

My family identified itself as Creole, a term that's always had ambiguous meanings. Unlike "African American" or "Black," Creole does not refer to physical appearance or African lineage. "Creole" was originally associated with immigrants from France, Spain, and Portugal living in the West Indies. More specifically, the term

Tina's parents, Mary Ann and Charles Ricard

referred the servants or slaves in the master's household, but over time it took on a wider meaning.

Even before the Louisiana Purchase, in 1803, "Creole" in Louisiana could mean White people, Black people, or people of mixed race. After 1803, when Louisiana became part of the United States, there was an influx of people from other states. Creole came to be a historical rather than a racial designation. Longstanding Louisiana residents called themselves Creoles to separate themselves from the Anglos who were newly arriving in the area.

To say you were Creole meant you were not a newcomer. Whether you were White, Black, or in between, you had been in the area for a long time. You could also speak the unique Louisiana Creole language. Creole was a term of hereditary pride, comparable to White families who could trace their lineage back to the Pilgrims on the *Mayflower*.

My father was a carpenter by trade, but he was really a builder in the broadest sense of the word. He worked for some good friends of the family who owned a construction company. They would come back from hunting and would empty a sack full of rabbits that would cover the whole floor. We'd go across the bayou. That was life in the country.

My father built our house from the ground up. My grandmother lived next door. Tina was my nickname in the family. My real name is Mary Leontine, which is a combination of grandmother's name— Leontine—and my mother's name, Maryann.

Our house in Baton Rouge was basic. When you entered, there was the front room. That's what it was called. There wasn't anything like living rooms and bedrooms. Beds could be in any of the rooms in the house.

In Louisiana my world seemed small. I was protected, or maybe even isolated. I wasn't really exposed to much in the city of Baton Rouge. There wasn't an urgent reason for me to be exposed to Baton Rouge, because under segregation there wasn't a lot for me to do there. Going to a movie at the Lincoln Theater meant sitting in the balcony because downstairs was "White Only." The popcorn concession was also only for Whites.

If I rode the bus, where I could sit depended on how many White people were riding. There was a sort of wooden marker that attached to the back of a seat on the bus. Non-Whites could only sit behind the marker. As more White people got on, the marker was moved toward the back, so if it got all the way back there was no place for me to sit.

That's just the way it was, a fact of life. I never really questioned it. My own family felt very safe and loving, even though we were poor in financial terms. My parents were both Catholic and I was raised in a Catholic environment. I went to Catholic school. It was a segregated school, of course, but it was very disciplined and proud. As far as personal contact with White people was concerned, I never really had much of that until we moved to California where I went to public school. There were just no White people in my world.

Arizona Street, where we lived, was mostly gravel. Home was a little shotgun house with three rooms. My parents slept in the living room in a fold-out sofa bed. In the adjacent room were two sets of bunk beds for my brothers, my sister, and me. There was also a small bathroom and a kitchen. There was no central heating, and certainly no air conditioning. I always walked to school until my mother learned to drive.

Many of my relatives passed for White, especially on my mother's side of the family. They were living as White people, so they avoided associating with me or my siblings. Lots of Creoles did that. Even today, Creoles consider themselves to be distinct and separate from African Americans. When I began attending an integrated school in Los Angeles, some of the White kids looked like my relatives. If I had a more conventionally African American appearance, I might have felt more uncomfortable.

I learned to swim at Brooks Park in Baton Rouge, which was a Black swimming pool. On the day I arrived for swimming lessons, I overheard the lifeguard talking. He said, "Oh, we have a 'high yellow' here today."

High yellow? It was the first time I'd ever heard that. It was a slang reference, and an uncomplimentary one, about the color of my skin.

This was something that Harold and I both experienced early in our lives. We did not see ourselves as White, but sometimes Black people did not see us as Black either. Light-skinned Blacks have always been privileged, a belief that goes back to plantation days. This is an issue that is rarely brought up in the mainstream media.

While everybody saw a distinction between Creole and White, those categories meant different things to different people. The Whites considered the Creoles to be Black. Creoles could not go to segregated public schools. My Catholic school was also segregated. There were no Whites, including teachers, but there were non-Creole Blacks. Of course, no people of color whatsoever could ride in the front of city busses or sit downstairs in movie theaters.

I believe the resentment against Creoles was racist, but it had some basis in fact. Light-skinned African Americans were received more readily in the White world. People with lighter skin were sometimes also granted higher status even by Blacks and Black organizations such as sororities and fraternities.

I certainly never felt privileged, but I didn't feel underprivileged either. We didn't have television in our house, so we didn't know how we were supposed to be feeling. At Christmas, I was lucky if I got one small doll, and I was glad to get it.

Although my father had certainly experienced discrimination, he never spoke about it, just as he never spoke about seeing death in the war. He was, of course, in a segregated army unit. When the Supreme Court's landmark decision in *Brown* vs. *Board of Education* came down, in 1954, the concept of "separate but equal" in schools was invalidated. I was, of course, too young to understand the significance of this, and we did not have a television to watch the news. Despite the importance of the Supreme Court's ruling and all the other milestones of the early civil rights movement, nothing much changed in Baton Rouge.

My interactions with the world beyond school and family were limited. Mostly I saw my cousins, who were Creole like myself. I had no Black friends, and I certainly had no White friends. In 1957, when President Dwight Eisenhower sent a thousand federal troops to integrate Central High School in Little Rock, Arkansas, I was unaware that anything had happened. For better or worse, my world was about my school and my family, within the limits of the Deep South environment.

A big step for my father—and our whole family—occurred in 1960 when he left for California by himself. The plan was to get established in Los Angeles and then bring the rest of the family. We all permanently left Louisiana in 1962, and the change was difficult for me. When we got to Los Angeles and were getting settled in, my parents reprimanded me for making long-distance calls back to Baton Rouge. But I was so homesick. The whole experience was a big adjustment.

Our first home in Los Angeles was a rented house on Seventh Avenue. My first school was Horace Mann, which I attended for one semester of ninth grade. Then I went to Washington High School for one semester, before my father bought a home on Ogden Drive.

After my short stay at Washington High School, I enrolled at LA High. I was the only one in the family who went there, because the school districts were soon redrawn and everyone else went to Hamilton. At the time, LA High was considered the flagship school of the city. It was also seen as a rich kid's school. "Bougie" was the word for it in the African American community: a bit snobbish and sheltered from the real world. Being at LA High meant that your family had money and probably the attitude that went with it.

Los Angeles High School was a huge place. Officially it was racially integrated, but it was still a segregated campus. The Blacks would be in one section, the Whites in another, and the Asians in a third. This seems to be what happens in large institutions with diverse populations.

It was unfortunate that there wasn't more interracial socializing, because the school was the only place where that could really happen. Since all the students lived in segregated areas of the city, there was no possibility of integrated friendships except at the school.

The church, along with school and family, was one of the foundations of my early life. Bible study was part of my experience with church, and, in fact, it still is to this day. Of course, what I read in the Bible as a child didn't have any day-to-day connection to my life at the time. Today, my experience of church and the Bible is different. I feel the power of my faith in "real time," so to speak. That power can explain so much, and events that might otherwise seem like pure chaos become pieces of a puzzle that, over time, become a recognizable and meaningful picture.

That's not all. Through the lens of faith, I can look back at my life and see how what happened can be explained and affirmed. Moving to Los Angeles from Baton Rouge, for instance, was a big leap into the unknown for me as a young girl. I sort of had an idea why it was happening, and I was excited about it to some extent, but I was worried about it too. I wondered why this move was happening now, but more than that, I wanted to know how it was going to turn out.

This is exactly the situation depicted in the twelfth chapter of the book of Genesis, in which God abruptly speaks to Abram (later called Abraham) and tells Abram to drop whatever he's been doing and head off in a new direction.

What direction? For what purpose? God doesn't say. He does say that when Abram follows this instruction, "I will make of you a great nation." But God doesn't say when or how this will happen. Abram was seventy-five years old at the time. He and his wife, Sarai (later Sarah), had no children, so another unanswered question was how God was going to make this elderly, childless couple the founders of a great nation.

But Abram does it. He just goes. He doesn't ask for more information. He doesn't ask for any guarantees. Maybe, by the age of seventy-five, he's learned that there are no sure things. So, he takes action, and that action is entirely based on faith. It's not logical. It's spiritual.

When our family moved to Los Angeles, no one sat me down and gave me a sermon about the Biblical reference points for what was happening. I probably wouldn't have understood that anyway. But today I can see how Abram's experience of "destination unknown" was the foundation of everything that came afterward in the Bible. More importantly, I can see how that experience never really ends, not for Abram, not for me, and not for anybody. Over and over, throughout our lives, we're always going into a strange land.

Sometimes that land is called Los Angeles, sometimes it's called parenthood, and sometimes it's called starting a new business. It's always somewhat scary, but my faith is what guides me. Although I wish I'd had that faith when I was much younger, I'm grateful that I have it now.

CHAPTER 2

THE GRACE TO BE UNDERESTIMATED

Commit your work to the LORD,
and your plans will be established.

—PROVERBS 16:3

For many years, when White Americans thought of the West, Black people were not in the picture. While a lot has been done to correct that misunderstanding, it's still being made every day in one way or another. White people may realize there were Black cowboys, but the presence and influence of Blacks in the cities of the West is largely unknown.

African Americans have lived in Los Angeles since the founding of the city, in 1781. There have been periods in which the African American population grew very rapidly, although the Black population has always been smaller than other racial minorities. To some extent this benefitted African Americans in Los Angeles, as race prejudice was deflected onto other ethnicities. There have been race riots against Latinos, and in the 1940 there was hostility to the

Japanese Americans, who eventually were transported to intern-ment camps.

From the beginning, growth of the Black population has, of course, been linked to economic opportunity, sometimes at the expense of other groups. In 1903, for instance, in an early example of Black and Latino tensions, a strike by Mexican American railroad employees was broken when the Southern Pacific Railroad brought in approximately two thousand Black workers.

In 1920, a census reported 15,579 African Americans were living in Los Angeles, mostly in the South-Central area of the city.

Twenty years later, owing to the growth of manufacturing, the Black population was 63,774—with approximately one hundred forty thousand more African Americans arriving during the manu-facturing boom of the 1940s war years. By 1950, the Black population was estimated at one hundred seventy thousand, and by 1960 Los Angeles had the fifth largest Black population of any city in America.

Beside the opportunities in manufacturing and other industries, Los Angeles has always been associated with the entertainment business—first, motion pictures, and later television.

The early silent film industry began to relocate from New York to Los Angeles in the first years of the twentieth century. The move was motivated mostly by the California sunshine, which expanded the possibilities for outdoor filming year-round.

At the start, and for years afterward, the new industry provided virtually no opportunities for African Americans. Movies were tremendously popular across the country—millions of people attended them three or four times a week—but almost all the actors and crew members were White. If a story included a Black character, the part would be played by a White actor in Blackface.

A prime example of this exclusion occurred in 1915, with the release of *The Birth of a Nation*. This silent film, almost three hours long, was directed and produced by David Ward Griffith and starred the famous silent actress Lillian Gish. *The Birth of a Nation* is considered a technical masterpiece by literally everyone who has written about film. At the same time, it has been almost universally criticized as racist propaganda, since the basic plot is a celebration of the Ku Klux Klan during the years of Reconstruction after the Civil War.

Blacks in *The Birth of a Nation* are depicted as racist caricatures. As if that weren't bad enough, they're played by Whites. Whatever the content of the film might be, the casting of the film speaks for itself.

This does not mean that there was no such thing as a Black film industry in the early years. There just wasn't a successful one in Los Angeles. In 1916 the Lincoln Motion Picture Company was founded by Noble Johnson, one of the rare African American actors who regularly worked in mainstream White films. Johnson's ambition was to provide films for the Black audience that was otherwise being ignored—and to provide work for Black actors and production staff.

In its first year, the Lincoln Motion Picture company produced *The Realization of a Negro's Ambition*, a full-length, two-reel film about a Black man in the oil business. The movie was advertised as featuring "an all-star Negro cast." It's testimony to the lack of respect accorded to Black filmmakers that not a single print of this film remains. Within five years of its founding, Lincoln Motion Pictures went out of business.

A breakthrough of sorts for Blacks in film occurred almost twenty years later, when the hugely talented Hattie McDaniel won an Academy Award for her role in *Gone with the Wind*. But this too had its share of controversy. Even at the awards ceremony, Hattie McDaniel's table was segregated to the back of the room. Meanwhile, she was also criticized by Black intellectuals for playing the "demeaning" role of a house servant on a plantation. When Hattie

McDaniel died in 1952, her wish to be buried in a cemetery in Hollywood was denied by the owner because of her race.

By the time I was a small child in the late 1940s, the African American population in Los Angeles was dispersed across areas such as Watts and Compton, which were essentially created to house industrial workers before and during World War II. Neighborhoods such as West Adams and Jefferson Park were populated by the relatively small number of wealthy African Americans.

Within that number was a subset of men and women who had connected with the opportunities in Hollywood and the music industry that were finally opening for African Americans. The Sugar Hill neighborhood off West Adams Boulevard, named after a neighborhood in Harlem, was home to Hattie McDaniel, Ethel Waters, Ray Charles, Lionel Hampton, Little Richard, and the Nicholas brothers, still considered the greatest tap dancers of any era, during the years when Harold Nicholas was married to the actress Dorothy Dandridge.

Growing up around Black actors, musicians, athletes, and other creative people made a lasting impression on me. It did influence what I wanted to do in my life, but that did not mean I wanted to be exactly like them.

I was raised during a vibrant period of growth in America and especially in Southern California. Growing up, I was unaware of racial injustice in the past or present. New visions of mobility and possibility had taken hold of the American psyche, setting forth a mass migration from East to West. For African Americans, there had already been a 1940s migration to Southern California for workers in the defense industry. Now, in the postwar era, men returning from military sought the rewards of a better life for themselves and their families.

It was a period when the automobile industry transitioned from manufacturing tanks and trucks to making cars that were affordable to millions of families. Just as this was happening in the late 1940s and 1950s, the Interstate Highway System was being built. Originally this was intended to facilitate military transportation, but it was quickly adapted to large-scale civilian use. All this and more set the stage for massive social transformation.

A significant number of migrating Americans headed for Los Angeles, a city built on the promise of opportunity. Jobs were abundant through military contracts in the airplane industry, in shipping and warehousing, in construction, and in dozens of other growing enterprises.

Los Angeles was a place where fantasy could appear to come to life. The city was a synthesis of imagination and reality seen through a rosy lens. The climate was months of blooming bougainvillea, roses, and fruit trees. It was no wonder that thousands of families packed their Studebakers, Chevys, and Fords for the cross-country drive to the golden land. It was a place where ordinary people could build comfortable lives, and the G.I. Bill made home-ownership affordable.

Boom and sprawl followed. Houses went up seemingly overnight. Anyone who could use a hammer or a trowel found work and made a good wage. Among them were my father and Uncle Wilbur. Returning soldiers from World War II, both equally ambitious, they saw the vast potential in construction and formed a company specializing in lathing and plastering.

My mother, Betty, had left home at age seventeen, partly to escape her father, who was both mentally and physically abusive to her. She moved in with her sister, who had left home a few years earlier and was now married. This was in 1942. My mother took a job on the assembly line at Douglas Aircraft. After the war, she took a job at Golden State Mutual, a Black-owned insurance company.

A huge building boom was in full force in Southern California, and work was plentiful for my father, Harold Lewis Sr., at Lewis

Brothers Inc. The company was unique among family businesses at that time, as it was an African American enterprise. The brothers were Black, as were most of the men they employed.

In addition to subcontracting their labor to developers, the company constructed houses and apartments independently for the extended family. That group included my mother and myself; my dad's seven brothers and five sisters, plus various wives, husbands, and their children. He knew then that owning real estate, and especially your own home, was the path to security.

Our family lived at 3942½ Montclair Avenue, a great location not far from the Sugar Hill neighborhood. On the ground floor, in the rear, were the offices of the construction business, where my mother kept the books and prepared the payroll.

The home was a disciplined environment, but the discipline was cooperative. The company and the family were two parts of the same whole, and the dominant element depended on the time of day. We were a domestic family from 5 p.m. to 5 a.m., and the from 5 a.m. to 5 p.m. it was all about business. My father and his six brothers often worked from early morning into the dark of night, and they provided well for the whole extended family.

Standing six feet four inches and weighing two hundred forty pounds, my father ruled over his enterprise with a firm but fair hand and an unshrinking gaze. Under the supervision of my father and Uncle Will, no one shirked their duties. Even brothers Ralph, Billy, Robert, Sam, and Jerry weren't exempt from the unbending expectation of hard, efficient work.

My father had seen action during the war in Europe. Like so many veterans, he kept his experiences private. From pictures that remain of him, he was a man confident in himself and sure of the future. One photo captures him standing with me at the front of the family home, my father's face beaming, his large dark hand resting

*Harold's parents,
Harold and Betty
Lewis*

softly on my shoulder. It's an image of a proud dad looking shyly at the camera, completely content.

My father preferred to avoid the grittier side of the business and took on the role of outside partner, negotiating contracts and dealing with clients and building permits. Uncle Will handled the day-to-day business, estimating jobs and bidding them, ordering equipment and supplies, assigning men to the various job sites, inspecting their finished work, leaving a bottle of scotch in the box where the inspectors would go to sign off on the work progress inspection cards.

Will Lewis was a master at bidding and ordering supplies. My father, on the other hand, was a visionary of sorts, overseeing the transformation of ideas and drawings into houses and buildings. But for Uncle Will, and for my father and everyone else in the family, the final objective was the same: to leave not even one shovelful of unused sand.

Everything suddenly changed when I was seven years old. My story and what I've learned of life, of fatherhood, and of business might be quite different had it not been for one night's shocking events. My mother woke me to say that my father was sick.

Even now I can still feel the shock of going into the bedroom and seeing my father lying on his back with his eyes closed. He didn't seem sick, just very still. But when I lifted one of his eyelids, I saw a blank lifeless stare.

That night and for many nights afterward, even though I knew my father was dead, I understood it only in a material sense. Even when I saw my mother—who was twenty-eight at the time—suffering the pain of seeing her husband at rest at Angelus Funeral Home, on a bed too short for him, I didn't immediately didn't feel the full impact of our loss. Today, I can recall only a few memories of personal contact with him. I was just too young.

Funerals in Black churches are emotional. The congregation sees no shame in openly expressing sorrow. My father's funeral was no exception. He lay in the casket in full military uniform, the gold oak leaves of a major on his uniform collar.

The pews of the Apostolic Faith Home Assembly Church, a converted theater that accommodated six hundred people, were packed with family, friends, employees of the business, and business associates. Many were sobbing. Staring at the casket as it was moved to the front of the room, I finally and fully realized what this loss really meant.

My mother was on the left and my father's youngest brother, Jerry—only four years older than myself—was seated to the right as a line of mourners passed. When they closed the casket, and everyone began to leave the sanctuary, I really took in the truth of what had happened. I began to cry. I said, "I want my daddy, but I don't have a daddy anymore."

The word "fatherless" was not in my vocabulary. Still, I knew that I would go into the world without the joy and support of a father-son connection, a relationship I would discover only after I had a son of my own. When I returned to school after my father's death I had a deep feeling of embarrassment from not being like the other kids—not having a father—while trying to hide that I felt different.

But I did feel different. My father had died of a heart attack at the age of thirty-four, a young and successful businessman, a contributor to his community, an officer in the US Army Reserves. His passing had a long-lasting impact. Decades later, as I became paranoid about my health. I was worried not just for myself but also for my children and my wife.

Although I was left fatherless, I was fortunate to have the love of a mother who was devoted to me and the affection that an extended family afforded. My Uncle Will and Uncle Bill were like surrogate fathers.

My mother was a strong woman who was further strengthened by her faith and the family that surrounded her with unconditional love. After she and my father married, his family had drawn her in and embraced her.

Their support and love were multiplied a hundredfold after my father died. That and her faith in God gave her the strength to go on.

The absence of fathers in contemporary Black families is often cited as a powerful negative influence, and correctly so. Children raised without a live-in father, for example, have a radically elevated incidence of teen pregnancy and of failure to attain a high school degree. I am grateful to my family, and especially for my mother's strength and courage, in not allowing that stereotype to apply to me.

Even commentators intending to debunk what they consider to be a myth of absent Black fathers cite statistics that attest to this reality. In 2016, approximately 2.5 million African American fathers lived with their children, but there were also 1.7 million Black fathers who lived apart from them. In 2010, 72 percent of Black children were born to unwed mothers, in contrast to the 24 percent cited in the well-known 1965 study by Senator Daniel Patrick Moynihan.

Although I was without a father, and although he saw his fair share of dangerous and unlawful behavior by some of his friends, I had some important advantages. By today's standards, I grew up in an environment of peace and prosperity. Part of that area was called "the jungle." That was a reference to its lush vegetation. It's still called the jungle, but now it's because of drugs and gang violence. Those elements were present when I was young, but not in today's epidemic form.

Even so, I was considered at high risk for failure. Throughout my education, I was given a discouraging view of my potential. My high school counselor suggested that rather than thinking about college, I should join the military or go to work for the post office.

It's difficult—but important—to rise above lowered expectations. If you allow others to set your limitations, you might as well stay where you are.

CHAPTER 3

THE TIME AND CHANCE OF LIFE

So, do not fear, for I am with you; do not be dismayed,
for I am your God. I will strengthen you and help you;
I will uphold you with my righteous right hand.

—ISAIAH 41:10

Growing up in Los Angeles, I was close to many of the best-known Black personalities in the entertainment industry. No one was a bigger celebrity than Sugar Ray Robinson, who even today is often credited as the greatest boxer of all time. It was truly a once-in-a-lifetime opportunity for me to become close to this larger-than-life personality. I have so many memories, and I learned so much. Through Ray, I was able to meet people from the top levels of sports, business, and entertainment, and to see them in their natural habitat. What I saw wasn't always pretty, but it proved to be useful.

Ray Robinson's only serious competition as "the Greatest" in the sport of boxing would be Muhammad Ali. But based strictly on their accomplishments in the ring, there really is no contest. Ali had a total of sixty-one fights, while Robinson had two hundred. Ali had an overall win rate of 91 percent against Robinson's 86 percent, but most of Ray's losses came at the end of his career when he was long past his prime.

Ray Robinson at one point had a professional record of one hundred twenty-eight wins, one loss, and two draws, including ninety-one victories in a row. He won the middleweight championship five times. He also fought as a lightweight, a light heavyweight, and a welterweight, and in 1946 he won the welterweight world championship. He fought Jake "Raging Bull" La Motta six times and won five.

Despite his status as an athlete, or perhaps because of it, Ray Robinson was always in danger of joining a list of African American boxing champions who were unfortunate at best and sometimes genuinely tragic. Americans watched these men achieve the pinnacle of celebrity, and then saw them fall into the depths. Many people seemed to enjoy watching both those trajectories.

In the early twentieth century, Jack Johnson became the heavyweight world champion and held the title from 1908 to 1915. Throughout his career, Johnson was consistently matched against White boxers and those fights became showcases for the nation's racial tensions. In victory, Johnson was not perceived to be sufficiently humble, which fanned the flames of racist anger.

Johnson also married three White women. He was certainly White America's most despised Black man, and he paid the price. After a conviction for "transporting a woman across state lines for sexual purposes," Johnson left the country to avoid jail but eventually served a year in a federal prison. In 1946, he died in a car crash after speeding away from a North Carolina restaurant that refused to serve him.

Unlike Jack Johnson, Joe Louis was quiet and diplomatic. But racist antagonism against his public image was still there. Louis's wins in the ring—especially against the German fighter Max Schmeling, one

Sugar Ray Robinson and Harold

of Hitler's favorites—were celebrated like national holidays by Black Americans. But in many parts of the country, those celebrations had to take place behind closed doors.

Ray Robinson was more difficult to characterize than either Jack Johnson or Joe Louis. He was good looking, good natured, and hugely talented. While not exactly humble, he was genuinely charming and was usually photographed with a smile on his face. He wasn't quiet, but he wasn't loud either. He earned people's respect—White people's too—in the boxing ring, and when he stopped fighting, he was still seen as an athlete-aristocrat in America and around the world.

Sugar Ray had his final fight in 1965, the same year I graduated from high school. I have always felt that there are no accidents in life; people and opportunities appear at the right time. In 1965, Ray was ending a career and I was trying to find my own path. My relationship with Ray would be one of those opportunities that would change my life forever.

My Uncle Billy married Ray Robinson's daughter Ramona, so in 1969 Ray became part of the family. I met Ray at the wedding and saw him at family gatherings afterward. Ray had virtually no relationship with his two sons. I was in college at the time, and I soon became a kind of substitute or surrogate progeny for Ray.

What followed during the next year was a chance to see the benefits as well as the vulnerabilities of life as a major African American celebrity.

Millie, Ray's third wife, was always reluctant to fly. When Ray had a trip coming up, she said to me, "Why don't you go with Ray?" Before long I was accompanying Ray pretty much wherever he wanted to go, whether it was to the gym nearby or to a public event across the country.

Once Ray had a meeting with Leonard Firestone, the heir to the tire company fortune who was also a prominent Republican, a former ambassador, and a well-known philanthropist. All in all, Leonard Firestone was a major big shot. Ray was hoping he would become a donor to Ray's youth foundation.

When Ray and I arrived at the building where Firestone had his office, we learned that the office was almost twenty floors up. This was a problem because Ray had a phobia of elevators. If an office were on a lower floor, Ray would take the stairs, but he was not going to walk up twenty flights. We requested that Firestone come down to the lobby—which he did. At that time few people in the world could have made such a request to Leonard Firestone, much less receive agreement. But Ray probably never saw this as a request. It wasn't an order, it wasn't a demand, but it was a confident expectation.

Even as a teenager, I had always felt that being on time was important. Time was also important to Ray, but in a different sense. Once he and I had arrived at the location of a noon meeting a few minutes early. I thought this was a positive development. Ray saw it differently.

"We definitely can't be early," he said. "In fact, we should be a few minutes late. When you're a celebrity, you should never be on time because you're always so busy. That's what people expect, so let's not disappoint them."

Ray was very much at home in his celebrity. Throughout his career he knew the power of his success. He was in high demand in an era when people formed long lines waiting for autographs from movie stars or athletes. People wanted to be around him, wanted to say that they'd talked with him, or even to say they knew him personally.

A number of celebrities had amateur boxing careers. Bob Hope, Barry Gordy, and even the gangster Mickey Cohen had tried their hands at the sport. They loved the game and Ray provided them the vicarious experience of being a champion, which they had never been able to achieve in real life.

The era of gangland influence in boxing at that time was in full force. Mickey Cohen was rumored to be heavily involved in the fight game. Ray, however, was never known to be subject to mob influence. At one time, Ray had an entire block of businesses in Harlem. These included a restaurant and a nightclub where celebrities mingled with some shady characters. But it was understood that Ray was not to be approached about any illicit activities.

People who wanted to know Ray personally—or wanted to claim to know him—did include Mafia types who had influence in the boxing world. Sometimes fights were fixed, even major ones, but Ray was given immunity from that kind of situation. Lucky Luciano, probably the most powerful man in the New York underworld, respected Ray and made sure he got respect from other people as well.

Luciano knew Ray from Ray's New York days. When Ray was in the area training for a fight, Luciano often called. He would, like any friend, ask how training was going. He would ask about Ray's wife. These were friendly exchanges. They weren't about "business."

The taboo of trying to fix a Ray Robinson fight was once violated by some small-time gangsters prior to the highly anticipated first match with Rocky Graziano. Ray was doing roadwork at his training camp in the mountains when he was approached by two men. They wanted Ray to lose the first fight. The rematch would also be fixed, but this time Ray would win. Then the third match would be open to the best fighter. For this Ray would be paid one million dollars.

It was never suggested that Graziano knew anything about this. Ray was the key person since he was the champion and was highly favored to win.

Ray was always a bit naïve about these matters, especially since he knew that he was protected by the gangster higher-ups. He simply laughed at the two men and started out to continue his run. But as he turned to leave, the men suggested that they could convince him if they had to, and they referenced his wife.

A few days later Ray got one of Lucky Luciano's calls, checking in on him. At some point in the conversation, Ray shared his encounter with the two men at his camp. Lucky told Ray to forget about it because those were just a couple of small-time hoods. The conversation ended as usual, with Lucky wishing Ray good luck.

Ray read the New York newspapers every day throughout his life. Not long after he spoke with Lucky, he sat down to read the paper and saw an article about two men found in an alley in New York, killed "gangland style." As he read further, he realized these were the men he'd seen at training camp.

Some weeks later, and longer than usual, Ray heard from Lucky Luciano again. Ray mentioned their earlier conversation about the men who had approached him about fixing the Graziano fight. After a short pause, Lucky said, "Now, Ray, you know the Bible says that tomorrow is promised to no man. How is training going?"

On my first trip to Washington, DC, with Ray, we were accompanied by Vince, a friend of Ray's who had played semipro football and loved being around a world-famous athlete. He was a partner in a car dealership in Los Angeles. He had plenty of money and time, so he would spend as much time as he could with Ray.

One day Vince approached Ray for advice about managing a young fighter in the Los Angeles area who had real potential. Knowing how the game worked, Ray told Vince not to get involved. Ray explained that if the fighter did become a contender, his handlers would be contacted by people who would want to be partners. There would be offers that would be difficult to refuse.

Vince, however, did not take Ray's advice, and as the fighter moved up the rankings Vince was indeed approached by potential "investors." But Vince refused their offer.

Soon after this, Vince went missing. It would be weeks before his fate came to light. Finally, Vince's Rolls-Royce was discovered in a parking garage. When the trunk was opened, Vince was found dead with a bullet hole in his forehead. The murder has never been solved.

When Ray and I first met, Ray's boxing career was over. His financial condition was unstable, as it would be for the rest of his life. Still, Ray Robinson was an official world-class celebrity. Being around Ray was a chance to see what being a celebrity really meant—especially a Black celebrity in both sports and entertainment.

How did being a celebrity express itself in Ray's daily life? If there was something Ray was supposed to do, he had somebody else to do it for him. He was one of the originators of what's now called an entourage. It was really the lifestyle of a king.

Ray didn't have an alarm clock to get him up in the morning. Somebody was assigned to wake him up, and at one point that somebody was me. To his credit, Ray was not a person who liked to lay in bed all day. His training as an athlete had gotten him used to early rising. He liked to take a three-mile walk in the morning, so I would call him at 5:30 a.m.

It was the same way in Ray's business ventures. If Ray said he wanted to call a film or television producer, he knew I had memorized the phone numbers for his contacts. This was amazing to Ray, who could never remember the numbers. He would sometimes forget whom he was calling after he dialed.

Ray was simply not programmed to do much for himself outside the boxing ring. Even just before a match, he would often go to sleep on the rubdown table. His handlers would have to wake him up to start fighting. The fights themselves were so incredibly demanding physically and emotionally that when he wasn't fighting or training, he was like a computer in sleep mode. He largely stayed that way in the years after he stopped boxing. He had a relaxed, almost cavalier personality.

Ray lived in Paris off and on for ten years. He learned to speak fluent French, and he would do shows at the famous Lido nightclub in Paris. He had his pink Cadillac shipped to France. Even though he spoke French, his entourage included an interpreter—as well as a golf pro and twenty or thirty other people.

Of course, women flocked to him regardless of his age or their age. Race certainly didn't matter to Ray, but people around him often had different expectations. Once he was involved in the creation of a TV sports quiz show. When Ray appeared for a meeting with the producers, one of the secretaries was literally all over him. She would sit on Ray's lap every time we went to their offices. As usual, Ray took this adulation for granted because, after all, he was the king. But I saw it differently.

After one meeting, I said, "Ray, the next time we come her, that girl will be gone. She's going to be fired." Ray seemed surprised. It was as if he couldn't understand why anything like that would happen. Of course, we never saw the secretary again.

Throughout his life Ray was oblivious to many racial issues, yet he was very aware of others. When he was in special services for the military, he and Joe Louis were scheduled to do a boxing exhibition somewhere in the South. Ray went out to look at the ring and noticed that a whole section of the seats was painted black. Obviously, this was where the segregated troops were supposed to sit. Ray immediately stated that he was not going to do the exhibition and returned to the barracks where he was staying.

It didn't matter to Ray that he was in the army and the event was supposed to be for the government. Ray was from the North and he had never been indoctrinated with the idea that racial segregation was just "the way things were." He reminded the base commander that his appearance had been arranged directly by the Pentagon. Immediately, the seating arrangements were changed to allow the soldiers to sit anywhere they chose.

While money was important to Ray, he saw it different than most people saw it. For many years it seemed like the money would never stop coming. Once, when Ray and Joe Louis were doing exhibitions to earn money while they were in the service, they gave their manager forty thousand dollars for expenses with a rubber band around it. Six weeks later, the manager handed them the rubber band. They had spent the entire forty thousand—the equivalent of four hundred thousand dollars today—in just six weeks.

Ray wasn't worried. There was a simple fix. He told the manager to set up another exhibition. Ray and Joe would take turns on the proceeds, so the next exhibition would be Ray's.

As Ray warmed up in the ring before the fight began, he heard a big ovation. He thought the crowd was cheering for him; it turned out to be for Joe Louis. Joe was coming down the aisle to take a front-row seat. On his arm was a gorgeous young lady wearing a full-length mink coat. As soon as he could, Ray asked Joe where he got the money for the mink coat. Joe answered, "Well, I took an advance on your purse."

Ray, Millie, and I went to Detroit around 1970 for the name change of Cobo Arena to Joe Louis Arena. Ray and Joe were very close, so it was natural for Ray to be part of the ceremony. As often happened through my connection with Ray, this would be an opportunity for me to meet people who would become an influence in my life.

Ray knew almost everyone at the event, including Berry Gordy, the founder of Motown Records. Barry was one of several friends who had been an amateur boxer so he, of course, admired Ray. Through Berry Gordy, Ray and I visited "Hitsville, USA," the home of Motown. For me, this was a lesson in what could be accomplished by an African American who was willing to put everything on the line. Berry Gordy represented the ultimate in creative and material success.

Early on the morning of the Motown visit, I had breakfast alone in the hotel coffee shop. Later, Ray asked if I had signed over the breakfast bill to the room. I said that I had just paid cash for it. Ray was indignant. "When we're on a trip like this, we don't pay for anything," he said.

This was the definition of celebrity entitlement: Celebrities don't carry any money—especially if, as was becoming the case with Ray, they don't have any money.

On another occasion, Ray visited a friend who owned Snyder and Sons, an upscale men's clothing store. The store did the wardrobe for Flip Wilson, whose show was one of the most popular on TV at the time. While talking with Ray, the store owner unexpectedly instructed his tailor to take my measurements.

Ray smiled knowingly, but I looked surprised. The store owner explained, "Look, you're with Ray all the time and a lot of people are going to see you. We want you to look sharp, and when they ask you where you got your clothes we want you to tell them Snyder and Sons." It was another lesson on the value of celebrity: free clothes.

After the visit to Hitsville, USA, Ray and I were invited to Berry Gordy's home. Barry was excited to see Ray and he led a tour of his home for us, which was another affirmation of his success. There was a billiard room, a bowling alley, and a putting green. An adjacent pool house was accessible from the main residence through an underground tunnel.

The Jackson Five had originally auditioned for Barry Gordy in the pool house, and they were staying with Barry when Ray and I visited. They were there to perform at the tribute. Everyone got acquainted over billiard games.

Another time, we went to Sammy Davis Jr.'s home. The purpose was to get some celebrities committed to a fund-raiser for Ray's youth foundation. It was an opportunity to see people like Quincy Jones, who had just released one of his first albums, in a relaxed environment. It seemed like the biggest stars were the nicest people. I'm sure it was because I was with Ray that they included me in the conversation, but I really felt accepted.

Ray Robinson was a proud man who took being a role model very seriously. Joe Louis, Nat King Cole, Sammy Davis Jr., and Ray himself had broken stereotypes and opened doors, and now they ought to pull others through. But he hated the way Frank Sinatra's Rat Pack treated Sammy.

Ray knew all those guys. Sinatra himself was another amateur boxer who idolized Ray. It was embarrassing when they would call on Sammy to tap dance—"cut a jig"—or make jokes at his expense. Ray knew they didn't mean anything by it, but he told Sammy, "You're more talented than any of them. Why do you let yourself be the joke all the time?"

Ray felt that Sammy accepted "being the joke" to stay in the group. However, the phrase "going along to get along" was not in Ray's vocabulary, and from then on it wasn't in mine either. At the same time, respect had to be earned as well as demanded. It's important to have pride in what you contribute, as well as in what you'll accept and what you won't.

Once, we attended a roast for Danny Thomas at the Friars Club. Ray was to be on the dais to take part in the roasting. The Friars Club had an exclusive all-White, all-male membership from the Hollywood A-list. Frank Sinatra, Milton Berle, Jack Benny, and George Burns were among them. When they arrived, Ray introduced me to Sinatra and others. It was a special treat. Edward G. Robinson told me, "Remember, you're a Robinson." He must have thought I was Ray's son!

Just before the program started, Ray whispered to me, "Don't ever forget why we're here. They always want something, and that's okay. We want something too. Just don't lose sight of that and make sure you get more than you give."

Being underestimated was one of Ray's best strategies. I saw Ray use it in every business meeting he was in.

In the early 1970s, Ray was always in demand by the media and could work as often as he liked. The producer of *Mod Squad*, a hot TV show at the time, called Ray with the idea for a show written for him. I attended a lunch meeting at the Brown Derby restaurant in Hollywood. Clarence Williams III, one of the stars of the show, was also there. The consensus from the lunch was that a show would be written just for Ray. A veteran TV writer named Mann Ruben would be doing the scripts.

The initial script called for Ray, who had retired long ago, to make a comeback with his old friend and opponent Rocky Graziano working his corner. A dialog coach was put on the show to help the two boxers. I was also assigned to help with this.

The group met for several weeks prior to the start of shooting. After a couple of days of rehearsal, both Ray and Rocky noticed that the coach and I weren't using their scripts. Rocky asked why this was happening. I had a simple answer: "We've been doing this so long we have the lines memorized." Both Ray and Rocky broke up laughing.

When shooting started, the director had set aside the whole first day for Ray to film just one scene. He would be on camera by himself, reciting ten pages of nonstop dialog. The scene was set up and the director called, "Action!" Incredibly, Ray went through the entire ten pages on the first take without a flaw.

The entire crew broke out in applause. Ray looked at the director and said, "How was that?" The director said, "Perfect." But he looked concerned. The entire day had been scheduled for the scene and now there was nothing to do. The next scene was not yet set up. Soon the entire lot at Paramount was buzzing about "one-take" Ray.

In 1966, Muhammad Ali was stripped of his heavyweight championship title when he refused to enter the draft. Ali had always admired Ray, and when he resumed boxing in 1970, he wanted to work with him as a mentor and as a training advisor. Ray liked Ali, but he told me that he was concerned about the effect of closely associating with Ali if Ali became a Muslim. Ray didn't have a problem with the Muslim faith, but at the time the country was very intimidated by anything that looked like Black militancy.

Because Ray felt that his career and credibility could be compromised if he openly connected with Ali, he became a kind of silent mentor. To announce the Ali-Frazier fight, a press conference was held at the Los Angeles Forum. When Ray and I came in, Ali called Ray's name and proclaimed that he, Ali, was a great fighter like Ray, was the only heavyweight that was light on his feet like Ray, and so forth. Then he announced that he was going to fight Joe Frazier.

After the press conference, Ray took Ali into a side room for a private conversation. I was also allowed in and was introduced by Ray. Then, in the private setting, Ray told Ali that a fight with Joe Frazier at that point was not a good move.

But Ali said that his trainer, Angelo Dundee, was sure that he was in great shape.

"Well, how many comebacks has Angelo had?" Ray asked. Ray reminded Ali that he, Ray, had five comebacks to the middleweight championship after layoffs.

He also mentioned Ali's reference to Ray and being light on his feet. Roadwork was not like staying on your toes and counter-punching in a real fight. He predicted that Ali's legs would be gone by the fifth round. When the fight happened, Ali was defeated after leaning on the ropes for most of the fight.

The next day Ray got a call from Ali telling him that he was right. His legs were gone, and the only thing he could do was lean on the ropes. But ever the marketer, Ali named his new tactic the "rope-a-dope," which he later used successfully in a championship fight against George Foreman. But at the outset, rope-a-dope was a necessity, not a tactic.

Through his connection with Ray, I was starting to get work in TV and film. It was the era of so-called disaster movies, like *The Poseidon Adventure* and *The Towering Inferno*. They were directed by Irwin Allen, the "master of disaster," who was developing a new film called *The City Beneath the Sea*. Casting celebrities was a motif in Allen's films, and Ray was going to appear in *The City Beneath the Sea*. Through Ray's connection with Allen, I got work as an extra in the film. He was in the union and it was a good way to make some money for two or three weeks of work. But was this the future I wanted?

It became clear to me that the industry had not yet moved far beyond the days of the stereotypical casting of Black actors. I gained some insight about this when Ray set up a reading for me for a picture that was being produced at Columbia Pictures.

The movie was called *Fat City*, with Jeff Bridges as the star. It was about an upcoming boxer, and there was a part for a young fighter who was going to compete against Bridges. Ray went with me to read for the producer. The reading went well, and I was also asked to do some shadowboxing, which I obviously had down. But I knew going in that the character and the dialog would not fit my look. The character was described as very dark skinned with a thick ethnic vocabulary. Neither my voice nor my being light skinned fit the part.

On another occasion, Ray and I had lunch with the producer of *Room 222*, a TV show about a high school teacher and counselor. The show was filmed in and around the high school that Tina and I had attended.

At the lunch with the producer, the conversation was about a new show entitled *Barefoot in the Park*. Ray was going to do a cameo. The female lead on the show was a light-skinned African American and I remarked that it would be nice to see more light-skinned Blacks getting roles. I mentioned my reading at Columbia and how I hadn't fit the description of the character.

The producer replied, "But you don't look Black," to which I responded, "How can I not look like what I am?" This was an "ah-ha" moment for him.

The following week I received a call from his office offering me the opportunity to work as a regular on *Room 222*. While this might have led to more opportunities for me, in the 1970s I knew the long-term chances were minimal. I enjoyed the experiences that I'd had but this was not an industry in which talent or even passion was enough to build a future—especially since there were few roles for

Blacks at that time. (As it turned out, years later I would circle back to Hollywood as a partner in a production company that would be completely Black owned.)

Ray had some sharp business people who worked on the board of his youth foundation. One of those advisers got to know me and Tina. She had worked at the foundation for a time.

One day he sat down with me and said, "I can see you've got potential in a lot of areas, but you don't really know what you want to do right now. Whatever you decide, don't totally devote yourself to Ray or the kinds of things he's doing now. Hanging around with celebrities can be exciting, but you need to figure out what you're going to do on your own. Ray has had his career. You've got to break away to start your own life. It's going to be hard, but you need to find your own path."

Ray was scheduled to go to Las Vegas to do six weeks of shows with Nancy Sinatra. He wanted me to go. "We'll find you something to do there," he said. But I declined. My time with Ray was over.

Today, I see what I did with Ray in the context of the celebrity culture that's exploded since the beginnings of the Internet and the constant presence of cell phones, Instagram, texting, and all the rest of it. So many African American boys want to be LeBron James. Girls can't get enough of Beyoncé. But those are realistic aspirations for virtually no one.

On the other hand, there are realistic aspirations for everyone, but they're not on the basketball court or the concert stage. I like to think of it this way: You're a big success when get a hundred-million-dollar check like LeBron James received. You're an even bigger success when you're the guy who has the money write that check. Ray once said, "I don't know if it's better to have had and lost, or never to have had at all."

CHAPTER 4

TAKING OFF

In the mid-1960s, an effort began in corporations to address the racial issues brought up by the civil rights movement. A friend of my family who was a radio talk-show personality was contacted by Gene Autry, the singing cowboy of the silver screen, who was now one of the most powerful businessmen in Los Angeles. Among other things, he owned several radio stations, and he wanted to bring some racial diversity into his companies.

At that time, being a radio DJ was one of the most prestigious and sought-after jobs among African Americans. It was a path to fame and fortune. But I was shown how to see beyond the myth and stereotype by a man named Lincoln Hilburn, who had lived in the same building we lived in, which my father had built.

Lin, who was an evening talk-show host at one of Gene Autry's stations, was given the task of putting together a program at the University of Southern California (USC) for recruiting and training Black men to become sales representatives in television and radio.

I enrolled in the class and upon completion I was offered a position with a radio station that was newly purchased from Wolfman Jack, one of the America's best-known radio personalities in that era. Wolfman owned the rights to a radio signal originating out of

Rosarito Beach in Mexico. Not governed by the rules of the FCC, the fifty-thousand-watt signal could be cranked up at night to two hundred fifty thousand watts. It could be heard across the country. As the Wolfman described it, "We had the most powerful signal in North America. Birds dropped dead when they flew too close to the tower."

I received very little on-the-job training. On my first day, I was given a rate sheet, a pat on the back and wished good luck by the sales manager. But with the instruction I received at USC and the confidence I learned from Ray Robinson, I handled the transition well.

Ray taught me to be confident even when I didn't feel confident, and to always give the impression you were in control and "belonged" even if you didn't. The ability to look people in the eye and speak convincingly to them could be like a poker game. The person who blinks first loses.

During the 1960s and 1970s, and even to this day, the excuse for not hiring or awarding contracts to Blacks is the absence of qualified candidates. As Lin Hilburn explained to me, debunking this racist excuse motivated and inspired Gene Autry to create a training program at USC. That training made me competitive in a White radio sales market in Los Angeles where there were only a few Blacks.

Less than a year after starting with Wolfman Jack, I was contacted by a Black executive who worked with the Westinghouse Broadcasting Company. Westinghouse owned the KFWB radio station that was looking for a Black sales representative. There was only a small pool of candidates, so my training and experience put me on the short list and Lin Hilburn recommended me for the position.

After an interview at the Ambassador Hotel on Wilshire Boulevard, I was offered the job. It was quite ironic that the interview took place at the Ambassador, which in the past had been a strictly segregated hotel. When Dorothy Dandridge did shows there, she wasn't

Hon. Ambassador Andrew Young with Tina and Harold

allowed to swim in the pool. Now here were two Black men having a business meeting in that very same hotel. Yes, some progress was beginning to happen.

KFWB was one of the top five stations in Los Angeles at that time and, unknown to me, this hiring was being handled by the corporate home office. The local sales manager had no say in the decision.

This made the process a little uncomfortable. A manager never likes to have anyone hired for him. In radio sales, when an opening comes up there is usually a list of clients to be serviced by the new hire. The new hire can bring income to the sales rep based on the commercial time sold to each client on the list. The sales manager quite naturally wants to hire the sales rep that he personally thinks will be the most effective.

But that would not be the practice in my case. During the first years of opening the mainstream workforce to Blacks, people felt threatened by sudden change. The problem was not necessarily that they didn't like certain individuals. It was more like, *what will this mean for me and my career?*

It was widely perceived—and it still is today—that any form of "affirmative action" was giving away jobs to minorities and taking them away from others. In fact, however, affirmative action only promised minorities an opportunity to interview. Companies could still hire the person of their choice, but they had to complete a form listing all the candidates they interviewed, including minorities.

In any case, I was hired. I was given a list of retailers I could call as a start toward building an expanded list for myself. As for my compensation, there was no exact figure, which was not the case with my counterparts. I was initially given a draw against future commissions. I didn't get a desk because there was no space available. A row of desks, already occupied, snaked around the perimeter of the office walls. Somehow some room was made for me near the sales manager's door. I had a card table, a phone, and a chair. I felt like I was in a time-out in grade school.

All this was clearly a slight to me, but to take offense would have been falling into the trap. Again, the lessons I had learned from Ray came to mind. I felt an obligation to him and so many others who had worked so hard to open the doors. I wasn't fighting for the middleweight championship, but I chose to see my job as a radio station sales rep as that kind of challenge.

I pounded the pavement for more than a year to build up a list of new clients. I couldn't revisit clients from my previous job because the price for spots was much higher here: fifty dollars per spot rather than twelve.

At that time, my mother was working at United Airlines as secretary to the regional vice president. I attended a charitable function and was introduced to United's regional sales manager, who seemed intrigued by my sales background. As it happened, United was at that time under a consent decree from the government to improve the number of minorities in management positions.

In the 1970s, United had some fifty thousand employees across the country, and few (if any) were minorities in the management ranks. In many companies, similar situations were blamed on the lack of college degrees among non-White personnel. This did not apply to United, however, because the chairman of the board himself did not have a college degree. It was his belief that if he could be a chief executive without college, he should not deny the same opportunity to others.

United's practice, therefore, was to hire people into non-management positions, such as ramp services or reservations, and then promote from within. From there, an employee could put in for promotion to management positions when they became open. But, as I had already seen happen on several occasions in my life, timing, experience, and divine intervention put me in front of United's regional sales manager when he was committed to adding Blacks to his sales team.

A deal was struck. If I would come to United, then I would be given a sales representative position. The only condition was that I would have to apply and start as a reservations representative. I would be trained to take calls and make reservations over the phone. I would have to stay in that position for six months, after which I could put in for a sales representative position that would be held open for me.

I decided to take this opportunity at United. As in radio, jobs were hard to get in the airline industry, which seemed rather glamorous. In addition, I had never really felt welcome at KFWB.

After I notified the station that I was resigning, the sales manager called a meeting. In a very sarcastic and condescending manner, he announced that, "given our commitment to hiring minorities, we will be looking to replace Harold with a Hispanic female. That way we can cover three categories at one time."

This was the state of American business after years of protest, civil disobedience, and even death for those who fought for people of color. I too had encountered my share of indignities, but I was fully aware of people who had endured much more. To honor them, I felt an obligation to stand up. So many others had never gotten this opportunity. Once again, I had learned a lesson from Sugar Ray: "Use the tool of letting people underestimate you if that's what they want. Believe in yourself and then take the next step up the ladder."

CHAPTER 5

THE SORT-OF-FRIENDLY SKIES

I was hired at United in February 1972. At the start, I was less than completely comfortable with my reservations job. I had always hated being in a sedentary position, confined to an office. But this was where I was now. I went through the few weeks of training focused not only on what I was learning, but also on how I could get off the telephone long enough to be promoted.

Once training was completed, I became one of approximately three hundred reservations agents in the Los Angeles office. It was a transition time for the airline industry, which had not recognized the number of minorities who didn't fly United, or didn't fly at all. This was a vast population that was not targeted in print, radio, or TV advertising. It was as if they didn't exist.

In contrast, White travelers, especially celebrities and frequent flyers, were catered to and given a high-profile VIP treatment whenever possible. A White celebrity would be met at the curb at the airport, escorted through baggage check-in, taken to a private lounge area, and then preferentially boarded on the plane. Black travelers got nothing like this treatment, not even Black celebrities.

As usual, this was not a conscious act of racism. It was a negligent oversight that developed from not knowing who the customers were, or who could possibly become customers. This ignorance was not exactly surprising, since there were no Black mangers in positions of influence when broad marketing strategies were put in place.

It so happened that I had met the Jackson Five in Detroit at Barry Gordy's home. They had recently moved to Los Angeles and had decided to stop flying United because they were refused entry into the Red Carpet lounge at LAX. When I became aware of this, I knew it was an opportunity to get off the phones in reservations by demonstrating how valuable the Jacksons, other Black entertainers, and Black travelers in general could be for United once the company woke up.

I went to the reservations manager and explained the treatment that the Jacksons had received. I also mentioned that the group was at peak popularity, traveling to more than two hundred destinations a year. And when they flew, they booked the entire first-class plus additional seats in coach for their band and opening acts. They also had about fifty thousand pounds of equipment for air freight. These were huge dollars for the airline that would now be lost because the Jacksons had been denied entrance to the Red Carpet lounge.

When I finished, the reservations manager had gotten the message. He asked what could be done to get them back. I explained that the Jacksons had to be treated like the VIPs and valued customers that they were. The reservation manager agreed.

After a pause, I said, "There' s one other thing. I have to travel with them to make sure everything goes smoothly."

To my surprise, the manager agreed. I was off the phones and on to this special assignment.

The first trip with the Jacksons was to Chicago for an annual Operation PUSH event where the group would perform with a few Motown acts. I knew the kinds of special perks that were given to celebrities and I went to work planning for the group. Motown as an organization liked Heineken beer for some reason. The Jacksons—and primarily Joe Jackson—liked chocolate chip ice cream and German chocolate cake. I called the flight kitchen and made sure all these items were made available.

By the day of the flight, all the arrangements had been made and the Jacksons' travel agent and road manager were informed. The group was met upon arrival at the airport and were escorted to the Red Carpet lounge while their baggage was handled. As the departure time approached, I went to the gate and had the group preboarded. This was how everything ought to be done. The Jacksons were pleased, and we secured their business from then on.

Now that the bar had been raised for Black celebrities, the next step was to expand awareness of minority travelers beyond the reservations manger and into the company's overall marketing and service. At the time I began my initiative with the Jacksons, I met Jo Moxley-Keita, who was also working in reservations. She had the idea of streamlining travel by Motown executives and performers through a private phone line to reservations. This would allow the tracking of dollars generated. It could build a case for being more inclusive to Blacks by showing the value of the Black traveler demographic.

United quickly became aware that this was a valuable segment of the traveling public that had not been identified. It wasn't long before the results of the revenue-generated tracking got to corporate headquarters in Chicago. By this time a colleague named Sheila Green had been working with Jo and me on what was called the "Something Special Desk," which Jo had started. The three of us were asked to fly to Chicago for a meeting with the marketing department.

While it was exciting that we had gotten the company's attention, I cautioned both Jo and Sheila that this meeting might not glean the results that we would hope for. We would probably be asked how this program could be expanded and what kind of marketing United should use to generate business in what was then called the Black Consumer Market, or BCM. I told Jo and Sheila that we should be prepared to give them everything that had brought the program to this point. But by the time a date was set for the meeting in Chicago, we had decided that if the point was just to pick our brains we would leave the meeting.

We arrived at United's headquarters in Chicago and were escorted to a large conference room. Soon two men entered, took seats at the far end of the table, and placed yellow legal pads in front of them. After we exchanged introductions, one of the men said that they wanted to learn more about the "Something Special Desk."

I began by asking the two men if they had anyone who was Black on the marketing team. I already knew the answer. They indicated that they didn't have any Black people on the staff.

I then stated that as reservations agents, we were being paid about seven hundred forty dollars per month. We were not being paid as marketing people. I knew they were making quite a bit more than that. But there was no point in trying to educate them on the Black experience or about how our low salaries were simply a continuation of what we had experienced throughout our lives.

I concluded by making it clear that we were not there to provide valuable information and then get lost. The only way we were going to work with the marketing team was by being members of the marketing team. We then excused ourselves, went back to the airport, and returned to Los Angeles. In retrospect, this was by no means a smart move. Fortunately, our bold move did not get us fired. The success of the program and the dollars that we brought to the company were what saved us.

I remembered what Ray told me: They want something from you. Just be sure you get as much as you give. Or maybe more.

The airline industry was seasonal at the time, and because I had no seniority I was furloughed. I returned to construction work during the furlough. After several months, I was called by United's personnel and offered the sales job I had been promised.

After I returned, several positive changes happened in the coming years. One was the creation of the Black Professional Organization (BPO), a network of Black managers in United Airlines to help employees share experiences and to prepare for opportunities as they came up. At the same time, United began an aggressive marketing campaign to draw Black travelers. This campaign included United ads, some featuring Black people in *Ebony*, which were now on the planes and on ethnic radio channels. A soul food option was available on in-flight menus.

When I received a promotion to sales. Jo and Sheila were also promoted to the sales office. This meant that the sales office now included three Blacks among a staff of thirty sales reps. Prior to this, there had been only one Black on that staff. His name was Gene Hines and he had been brought into sales from his position as a Sky Cap. Gene was basically assigned the minority business, such as it was. This mainly involved attending dinners sponsored by the NAACP and similar events.

The sales office took up half of the seventeenth floor of the Union Bank building, which United used as its Los Angeles headquarters. The sales office had rows of desks, as in a stock brokerage. The office was divided into three sections, each of which was responsible for a different area of Los Angeles.

I was in the same section as Gene, with my desk directly in front of his. As soon as I arrived in the office, it was apparent that no one had gotten the message about not telling jokes about Black people, especially in front of Black people. If Gene was uncomfortable with those jokes, he must have decided he just had to tolerate it.

But I was not going to tolerate it. When one of the salesmen turned to the group and began a joke with "Did you hear the one about the N word?" I stood up and said, "Stop right there. The next person who has a joke like that is going out the window."

This drew a deafening silence. But from that day forward the status quo of the office was radically changed.

Several years later, I was promoted to the personnel department. Today it's called human resources. There were four personnel representatives who handled all the Los Angeles employees. I was responsible for the reservations office, where I had started at United, and for the pilots and flight attendants. Again, I was the only African American. (By this time, Tina had left United and was an in-flight instructor for Continental Airlines.)

All in all, I was responsible for a total of twenty-five hundred United employees. Through the personnel office, I was able to interact with upper-management department heads. I was able to see, hear, and identify any individuals who had prejudices in hiring and promotion. Quite often, when you're the only Black person in the room, people forget that your Black and unconsciously reveal themselves. At times like that, keeping your cool is a special talent, especially if you're consistently reminded how "different" you are when openings became available for various positions.

I met with Black candidates and prepared them for interviews. I knew that the hiring process and the results of interviews could depend on who was asking the questions.

There was a manager of in-flight services who was partial, shall we say, to White candidates. On one occasion, I received a requisition from a flight attendant who wanted to transfer to Los Angeles from San Francisco. While "race" was not blatantly specified on the requisition form, ethnicity was coded with a number. This, in effect, identified the applicant's race.

When the flight attendant's requisition was given to the in-flight manager, he looked at it and frowned. Then he held it up and said, "There's a mistake here. It says this girl is Black."

I said, "Well, she *is* Black."

"She's too pretty to be Black."

I said, "She's Black and she's pretty too."

I could barely restrain my anger. To some extent he was hiding his racism behind clumsy humor. That was how those people protected themselves. It was what every Black person had to deal with in the White corporate world. It was not made any easier by the reality that if you were a Black person in management you were probably the only one in your department. They would be happy to find an excuse to let you go.

Like an inoculation that strengthens your immune system, like many Black people, I have been immunized to handle any situation to continue the journey. But handling a situation doesn't mean just giving in to it. My priority was always to stay in the game and eventually to win it. In the 1970s, getting fired was always an immediate possibility, and getting fired would not benefit anyone except the adversary.

The violent protests of the late 1960s were over. It was time for change from a different angle. This involved changing people's minds and attitudes in order to change behavior. When the personnel manager made that racist statement about the flight attendant's transfer request, I knew that any aggressive push back would be turned around to make me the bad guy in the corporate view. But that person had revealed himself. I was going to watch him and let him hang himself, and to make that happen I was going to assist him in any way that I could.

I knew I would always have to work around this manager to get him to do the right thing. When the industry created an in-flight supervisor position, this was an opportunity for five people to get very desirable jobs. It was my responsibility to provide candidates to the manager for his consideration. For the five in-flight candidates, I gathered six candidates, five Blacks and one White. I personally took the Black candidates off site to prepare them for their interviews.

Upon completion of the interviews, the manager called me to ask if I had any additional candidates. I responded that I had provided six candidates. If there was a need to see more, I would get back to him.

It was important to remember that United at that time was under a government consent decree about diversity in hiring, or at least about diversity in offering interviews for candidates. I met with my manager, Ed, who had authority over both me and the manager who was causing problems. I had an excellent relationship with Ed. I knew it was his personal mission to provide opportunities for minorities, whether we had a consent decree or not. He had a genuine desire to create a truly level playing field.

Ed knew what I was doing, and I knew that he knew. We never talked about it but if we looked at each other when these issues came up we just had an understanding.

I explained that I had given the manager six candidates, five of whom were Black and who were more than qualified. In fact, the single White candidate was nowhere near as strong as the others. I went on to say that if the manager didn't take the five most qualified candidates, the in-flight department would fall short of the diversity goals. Even more importantly, my manager and our office would not meet personal objectives.

Shortly after that meeting, the in-flight manager called Ed. He stated that he had asked me for more candidates. Ed asked if the five candidates I had already provided were qualified, and the manager had to admit that they were.

"Then hire them," my manager said. "You're not getting any more candidates."

Mission accomplished, at least in this case. But I was challenged by this manager at every opportunity. In meetings he would openly confront me. Sometimes he called me on the phone to ask an obscure question just to see if I knew the answer. Eventually he was fired.

While I was in human resources, I tried to make the most of my tenure by helping minorities advance into positions of greater responsibility and higher pay. This was not at the expense of the White employees for whom I was also responsible for. But since they already had a very effective old-boys' network, I wanted to provide as much as I could to new employees, including a support network for Blacks.

I've mentioned United's Black Professional Organization, whose mission was to help Black employees with advancement and other issues. At one meeting of the BPO, the president of United Airlines, Dick Ferris, was asked why so many management positions were filled even before they were publicly posted. A BPO member suggested to the president that this advantage might be the result of a network that knew about job openings before anyone else.

Dick Ferris was a Cornell graduate and always a straight shooter who had a Black male as his assistant. He said, "Well, it's clear to me that the Black Professional Organization is becoming the best network in the company. I urge you to use it and if you choose not to use it, that's your own fault."

Despite many problems, my years at United were great. The airline industry at the time was a desirable, exciting, and even a glamorous place to work. The industry was changing by the beginning of 1980s. Computerizationand consolidation were revolutionary influences. But some things were still not changing.

Before leaving the company, I had occasion to go through the file of an employee who had been promoted to a position that I was interested in and qualified for. The file contained a form regarding the government consent decree. It listed the candidates who had been interviewed for the position, and my name was included among those candidates. But I had never been interviewed.

This was the validation. It was about time to move on.

PART TWO

CHAPTER 6

FLIGHT ATTENDANT

For I know the thoughts that I think toward you,
saith the LORD, thoughts of peace, and not of evil,
to give you an expected end.

—JEREMIAH 29:11

No one can make you feel inferior without your consent.

—ELEANOR ROOSEVELT

From the mid-1950s into the early 1960s, a few hugely successful enterprises revolutionized America's business landscape. One of these was the National Football League. Professional football had existed since the 1920s, and its popularity had steadily grown, but it was still less prominent than college football, and much less than Major League Baseball.

Then something happened that caused radical change. The NFL's championship game in 1958 between the Baltimore Colts and the New York Giants was a close game that went down to the final minute before Baltimore won.

Tina in United Airlines Uniform

But there had been games like that before. The difference was that this game had been televised, and lots of people now had televisions. The close game sparked interest in pro football, but perhaps more importantly, it sparked interest in television. Following the game, sales of television sets immediately spiked. Professional football and television began a symbiotic relationship that continued and grew in the coming years, particularly when Coach Vince Lombardi was building his dominant teams in Green Bay, Wisconsin. That was a golden age for NFL football, and it was also a golden age for network television. Advertisers would pay whatever it cost to showcase their products during the Sunday games.

Playboy was another 1950s phenomenon. Now, more than sixty years later, the huge popularity and impact of *Playboy* has been largely forgotten in the permissive twenty-first-century environment. But in its time *Playboy* was both revolutionary and profitable. In its peak years, *Playboy* was able to pay its monthly expenses entirely through over the counter retail sales. Advertising and subscription revenues were pure profit. It's a safe bet that nothing like this will ever happen again in commercial media.

A third game-changing development was a technological innovation rather than a single company. This was the introduction of jet air travel, which changed everything. Before jet travel, for instance, it would have been difficult for Major League Baseball to expand to the West, where teams in Los Angeles and San Francisco would have been handicapped by the distance to Chicago or New York.

But if the connection between jet planes and professional sports was important, there was also a real connection between air travel and the *Playboy* vibe. The stewardesses, later called flight attendants, expressed a glamorous attractiveness that was diligently cultivated by the airlines. In the postwar years, they were, of course, all female, and for most of that time they were also all White.

In one way or another, all these societal changes affected millions of Americans—and I think it's fair to say that they affected me more than most.

After my family arrived in Los Angeles, we moved twice, so I attended two different middle schools. Then I went to Los Angeles High School, considered one of the best in the city. It was picturesque and dignified. The school's exterior was used in the *Room 222* television show.

In 1967, I enrolled at Los Angeles City College. Unlike Los Angeles High School, picturesque and dignified were not adjectives that would apply to LACC. It was a wild time, certainly a different world from Louisiana.

Moving from Louisiana to Los Angeles had caused me to develop a new inner strength. I have always been a fast learner, and I became a totally different person. People could not believe that I was from the South. I developed a militant perspective and I pushed back hard at the smallest hint of discrimination.

AT LACC, I was active in the Black Student Union. I didn't formally join any organizations, but I attended a Muslim mosque and some Black Panther meetings. Once a man stumbled into a meeting after being shot.

In 1972, my life took another turn when I applied to United Airlines to be a flight attendant. I was accepted and went to Chicago for training.

Coming from the South and being very much overprotected by my parents, it was a big leap for me to leave home and become a flight attendant. I had never been on an airplane before that first flight was from Los Angeles to Chicago. My parents were torn about my leaving home at all, and I was most likely going be placed in Chicago or on the East Coast. Their last words to me before I left were, "If you don't like it, you just come back home" Those words alone gave me more strength to succeed.

After completing training, I was based in Chicago and shared an apartment with two other flight attendants. After a year, she put in for a transfer to Los Angeles.

My base pay at that time was $530 per month. Not a lot, but perhaps not unusual at that time. And, of course, being a flight attendant was very glamourous, right?

In the beginning, it was not that way at all. Passenger air travel in the United States began in 1914, with so-called stewards filling the role that stewards had also played on oceangoing passenger liners.

They were all male at first. Before long, their responsibilities expanded into the medical realm as propeller-driven air travel became available, which was accompanied by air turbulence and passenger nausea. Male stewards turned into female stewardesses, who needed to have a nursing background. Sometimes the stewardesses even wore nurse's uniforms.

The woman generally credited as the first "modern" flight attendant was Ellen Church, of Iowa, who was hired in 1930 by United Airlines, with credentials as a nurse and also as a pilot. She could not be hired as a pilot, but United drew on her nursing background to market the safety of flying.

As flying became less turbulent with the advent of higher-altitude jets, the medical responsibilities of flight attendants diminished, but other requirements remained. In the 1960s, retirement for stewardesses was mandatory by age thirty-two. Marriage or pregnancy meant automatic disqualification. A 1966 want ad for Eastern Airlines stewardesses stipulated:

High school graduate, single (widows and divorcees with no children considered), 20 years of age (girls 19½ may apply for future consideration). 5'2" but no more than 5'9", weight 105 to 135 in proportion to height and at least 20/40 vision without glasses.

Ruth Carol Taylor, who was hired by Mohawk Airlines in 1958, was the first African American flight attendant to actually fly in a plane. But the way had been opened by Patricia Banks, who in 1957 brought a lawsuit for discrimination against Trans World Airlines, Mohawk Airlines, and Capitol Airlines. She was eventually hired by Capitol in 1959.

Yet a legal victory was certainly not the end of discriminatory hiring, or of racism against flight attendants who had finally managed to get hired.

And racism wasn't the only prejudice that was on the surface. Sexism wasn't even a word back then, but there was plenty of sexism for flight attendants. The hiring process was like purchasing a race horse. Here's the text of a radio ad that was broadcast in the late 1960s:

PSA, the airline that is famous for its stewardesses, is looking for girls. Yes, girls to fill a cute orange mini-uniform...girls who smile and mean it...girls who give other people a lift. If you're single, 18½ to 26 years old, 5 feet 1 to 5 feet 9, 105 to 135 pounds, have a high school diploma or better, then come in for an interview at the Los Angeles International Airport.

An ad like that could bring in more than ten thousand applicants for a flight attendant's job. The number would immediately be screened down to a thousand. A hundred women would then make the cut for a final interview, and ultimately ten might be hired.

Even after you were hired, you were screened before every flight and you had to be perfect. There was a weight check, a uniform check, and a hair check. If there was any deviation, you could be suspended.

But that wasn't all.

Once, for example, in my early days with the airline, I was bringing the food cart down the aisle. Passengers could choose chicken or roast or whatever else was on the menu that day.

One of the passengers, an older lady, said that she didn't want me to serve her. The reason was simple: I was not a White woman.

I said, "Well, I'm the one who's serving these meals on this part of the plane. If you want to eat, I'm the one who will be serving you." But the woman was adamant. She wanted a White server.

I was the lead flight attendant on this flight, which meant I was in charge of the others. I went to the other flight attendants and said, "If she doesn't take the food from me, she doesn't eat." When she requested a meal from the other flight attendants, they said the exact same thing to the passenger. "She will serve you, or you don't eat."

So, the passenger didn't eat. That's how things were in those days. Even very blatant racism could be right there on the surface.

I was a flight attendant in Los Angeles when I met Harold in 1974. It was at his birthday party, where I was a guest. He never called me.

A full year later, I was in LA for a day visiting a friend. Harold drove by, headed to see Sugar Ray, who lived a few blocks away on the same street. When we saw each other as he passed, he turned around and we exchanged numbers again. And he asked me out to dinner.

Not long afterward, I was asked to participate in *Ebony*'s Fashion Fair tour representing United Airlines. But since I was dating Harold, I turned down the opportunity. Three months later Harold asked me to marry him. It was fate that Harold had been driving down the street at that exact time, on his way to Sugar Ray's. Five minutes' difference either way and we would never have married.

Harold and I were both working for United Airlines when a strike took place. Because the strike originated with the mechanics, everyone was out of work, including flight attendants. The strike continued for three months, during which no one was getting paid.

Harold did not participate in the strike because his job in human resources was a management position. He was working at the airport a few days before Christmas when union reps drove up in a luxury limousine and told the striking mechanics to "hang in there." Meanwhile, whether he was management or not, Harold was put on half-pay once the strike had gone on for thirty days.

Strikes were frequent in those days, which presented a real disadvantage for a married couple who worked in different areas of the same airline. Harold and I felt it would be wiser if both of us didn't work at the same airline, so in 1979, I left United and accepted a position with Continental Airlines, where I took a job as an instructor.

Six months after Jeremy, our first child, was born, I was working with four other instructors, as well as a manager. Before long, a merger of Texas International Airlines with Continental created redundancy in staffing, which led to some layoffs. I was the last remaining instructor when the other four instructors were let go. My manager also announced that she was getting married, and she too would be leaving the company.

I naturally believed that I would be promoted to the manager position. To my surprise, however, I was called in one day, told how valuable I was to the company, and then informed that I was being counted on to train the new manager. This new manager—a White male, as it happened—was coming in from sales without any in-flight experience. I replied that I would need to discuss the situation with my husband.

That night Harold and I talked about where we were now in our careers and where we wanted to go. As fate would have it, we had both hit the glass ceiling at the same time. Now we would do something else at the same time. We would open a business of our own.

CHAPTER 7

Dis-United

In 1982, I had been working at United Airlines for ten years. I had held management positions in sales, reservations, and human resources. I had also been identified through a management development program as a candidate for several upper-management positions. When one of these opportunities opened, I was interviewed for a position as assistant to the regional vice president.

This job was something that I had been preparing for in various management positions that I had already held. Coincidently, at this same time, Ronald Reagan was leaving the governor's office in California. As always happens at such times, people who had been in government administration began looking for jobs in the private sector. Along these lines, a high-ranking member of Governor Reagan's administration called United Airlines seeking a position for someone on his staff.

The position for which I had interviewed was given to the Reagan administration staff member, who was African American. That was a blow, since I had been getting ready for an opportunity like this for a long time and this was the only position of its kind in the region.

Harold

I had to make a big decision. How would I handle someone with no airline experience getting a job that I had been preparing for the last ten years? It was a moment that called for some soul searching.

Management opportunities for Blacks were rare anywhere in corporate America at that time and especially in United Airlines. My faith and my upbringing told me not to react with anger, especially toward the person who got the job. I didn't even know him. In addition, I had to be true to my commitment toward supporting African Americans gaining management positions, even if it came at my own expense.

Unfortunately, this was not even an uncommon turn of events. Because there were so few management opportunities, African

Americans often ended up competing for the same job. I decided to support Mel, the person from the Reagan administration, by sharing what I had learned about the company over the years. To do anything less would be to set him up for failure, since he knew nothing about the airline industry in general and even less about the politics and challenges for African Americans in United Airlines.

I chose to follow my faith by trusting that this was not my turn. I believed that God had a plan for both of us and I had to hold fast to that belief. When Mel started work, I took the initiative and introduced myself. Mel and I became friends. I was glad I gave him my full support, and I still am.

In the following months, the friendship between Mel and me would prove important for both of us. Before long, Ronald Regan began his run for the White House. With this development, another call came to United Airlines requesting that Mel be given a leave of absence to work on the future president's campaign. It was an example of why it was so important for companies to keep relationships with former politicians. Those relationships could come in handy later on.

Mel and I kept in touch during his leave to the campaign. Once Reagan was elected, Mel was selected to join the administration as one of the president's senior policy advisors. Although we were invited, Tina and I were not able to attend the inauguration. Later, we did connect with Mel, and I had the opportunity to visit the White House for a personal tour, and to dine in the executive dining room below the Oval Office.

By this time, Tina and I were committed to leaving the airline industry. The obstacles facing African Americans, both men and women, were changing but only at a very slow pace. The airline business was just not going to offer promotions to the management positions that would allow us to build the lifestyle that we wanted.

The industry in general was also changing. Texas Air Corporation disappeared when it was acquired by Continental and soon Pan American Airlines, Western Airlines, and others would also be no more. In this unstable environment, we realized that we wanted to build something of our own that we could hand down to our children. The only way we could do that was by having a business of our own.

We had some friends who were McDonald's franchisees, so we did some research on that company. At first, we suspected that this might be too big a leap for us. But we soon realized that being passed over for promotions in the corporate world was causing us to mistakenly question our skills. "You're not ready yet" is usually a mistaken message to take in, whether it's coming from yourself or from people around you. If you wait until everything is perfectly in order, you may be waiting forever. That might even be the outcome (or the excuse) you're secretly looking for.

We didn't commit to McDonald's at first. Instead, we chose to open a Sir Speedy printing franchise. As soon as we were accepted for a store, we applied for a bank-guaranteed loan whereby the bank would guarantee 80 percent of the balance and the government's Small Business Association (SBA) would guarantee 20 percent. Once the bank had approved its participation, the package was sent to the SBA for approval.

A few weeks later, the bank called to advise me that the SBA had turned down the loan. This caught us totally off guard, because we both had good jobs, owned our home, and had good credit.

When I asked the bank if I could speak directly to the SBA, I was told that would not be possible. The SBA would not talk to me because the bank was the conduit.

I was extremely upset when I got off the phone. For a moment, I was tempted to see this as the end of our entrepreneurial dream.

Fortunately, my faith remained steadfast and a new realization dawned on me. I contacted Mel, who had gotten the managerial position I'd wanted at United and who was now working in the Reagan administration. I had helped to acclimate Mel at the airline, and we had become friends. Maybe this was all part of some master plan—because if I had not befriended Mel, I would not have been able to make the call that I was about to make.

I phoned Mel at the White House. As soon as he came on the line, I made a joking reference to the Reagan-era slogan of trickle-down economics. "Mel," I said, "the economics is not trickling down."

Mel laughed and asked, "What's going on?" I told him the story about being turned down for the loan. With no hesitation, Mel asked if I would be at my desk at ten the next morning. I responded that I would be there.

The next morning at precisely 10 a.m. I received a call from a gentleman at the SBA. I asked why we had been turned down for a loan, and the man replied, "We looked at your situation, and we felt you were taking too much risk by quitting your jobs." I responded that I had not asked for career advice, but for a loan that we felt qualified to receive.

Almost immediately the man said, "Mr. Lewis, I completely understand, and your loan has been approved."

This reinforced my belief that you never know how an act of kindness or an act of faith will come back to reward you tenfold. Had I not befriended Mel when he got the position at United, that reward would never have come around. You don't sacrifice your principles for personal gain.

Tina and I opened our Sir Speedy franchise in 1982 in Los Angeles. This was a carefully planned decision. We were familiar with the area and did not want to be a small print shop in an outlying location. We were not interested in doing wedding invitations and business cards. We wanted to build a strong commercial business.

We also set up the business so that each of us had clear and specific areas of responsibility. Tina and I both had sales experience, but we felt that Tina's public contact experience as a flight attendant and as a pharmaceutical sales rep made her a far better salesperson than I was. Additionally, in the printing business most of the buyers are men, and Tina would certainly have greater success than I would at getting in the door and pitching our business. This was not exploitation. It was smart business practice. We knew we had to maximize our individual talents.

We would be working side by side, which could be a challenging proposition. In order to maintain our marriage, we would need a day plan and an evening plan. We decided that we should limit our business conversations to the office. After 6 p.m. we would only discuss personal and family matters. If we didn't do this, we would probably burn ourselves out and ruin our home life. We also had to consider our son Jeremy, who was five years old and needed our undivided attention at home.

Before we began classroom training for the business, we were fortunate to have spent some time with a married couple who owned a Sir Speedy that we had been spending time with prior to the classroom. This gave us a jump start on the real experience of the business, which was reinforced by the classroom work.

I would handle the operations. But since the training was disappointingly minimal, I needed to bring myself up to speed on operating the printing presses, cameras, and every piece of equipment necessary to run the shop. Really, the single most important requirement for the owner of any business is knowing everything that the employees need to know. Owners can never let themselves be held hostage by employees who feel that they are not replaceable.

Upon completion of the training, we began a search for a location with as much commercial business as possible. We chose a site near the Los Angeles airport for two reasons. The airlines, car rentals, and many commercial businesses were in that immediate area. We also knew the area after being in the airline business.

I got a call from my manager at Untied, saying he had heard that I might be looking to open a business. He had been surprised when I took a leave of absence, given my tenure with the company, and he was, of course, concerned that he would have to replace me if I chose to leave. When I asked where he got his information about my starting a business, he wouldn't say. I finally just told him that I would return at the end of my leave.

When the manager pressed me for more, I reminded him that I had been in human resources and had seen many leaves of absence like mine receive approval with no more questions asked. I even said I could provide a list of those leaves if he wanted one. He paused and said, "I'll see you when you get back." I wasn't about to let him intimidate me. I knew where the bodies were buried.

When we found a suitable location for our store, we began contracting for the buildout of the space. It would be several months before the full buildout was completed and the equipment was installed. I returned to work part time at United in my original position as a reservations sales rep.

Taking reservation calls was sometimes entertaining. When fare wars were going on among the airlines, we had so-called standby fares. Customers would wait at the airport for a cancellation, which would get them on the plane for a lower fare. One night I got a call from an elderly lady who wanted to know if the standby ticket meant she would have to stand by the seat for the whole flight, because she didn't know if she could do that. After I composed myself, I reassured her that she would be able to sit down for the entire flight.

The move back to reservations allowed me to work at Sir Speedy during the day and at United at night. It also allowed me to become tenured for my retirement benefits. I continued this for a year while we got the franchise established. Sometimes you have to take a step back in order to go forward.

Then we were finally ready to open our doors. We had hired an employee to run the printing press, and Tina began cold-calling companies to solicit their printing business.

The Bible speaks about two people being "equally yoked." I have never been a chauvinist and I have always hoped to show Tina the full measure of respect that she deserves. Perhaps this comes from being raised in a family where my mother and my grandmother and all my aunts were strong women in the best sense of the word. They carried themselves with dignity and grace and saw themselves as leaders rather than followers.

That wasn't a matter of ego. It was just fundamental self-respect. If there's one thing that's important in a relationship—and especially for a couple who are going into business together—it's the ability to put ego aside. Both of us understood that priority.

Many of our customers didn't know we were married. Sometimes someone would come in while I was in the back running the press. If Tina wasn't there, I would go up to the front with ink on my hands and up to my elbows to see how I could help them. They might hand me a check to pay a bill, but with a little hesitation because they didn't know if I could be trusted. They'd want me to assure them that Tina would get the check. I didn't take that distrust personally at all. I was just doing whatever needed to be done. Tina and I were partners in the business just as we were (and are) partners in our whole lives.

There were many high-rise office buildings on Century Boulevard, the main street leading into LAX. Tina would begin on the first floor and work her way through a whole building, knocking on every door. As business started to come in, she began calling on the airlines, and she landed Western Airlines, Pan American, and Continental. She also brought in Budget Rent a Car, Neutrogena, and many others. She was doing great and we were really a commercial house.

Los Angeles had been awarded the 1984 Olympic Games, and the Olympic committee was setting up offices. Tina began calling on the committee to solicit an Olympic contract. Day after day she contacted the public relations office, marketing, and whomever else she could think of.

One day Tina was on her way to the Olympic public relations office when a woman approached her in the lobby of the building. She looked right at Tina and said, "Printing, right?"

"Yes, that's right," Tina said.

The woman held up what turned out to be an acetate with a picture on it. She asked Tina, "Can you do this?"

"Yes, of course. Absolutely," Tina responded, although she really had no idea what kind of image it was or how it was produced.

She brought the acetate back to the office and showed it to me. After figuring out what it was, we farmed the job out since it wasn't anything we could do in-house. Tina very quickly returned the completed job and we began getting more work from the Olympic committee. Soon we had landed a contract for the duration of the 1984 games. The work included four-color reproductions of magazine covers from *Sports Illustrated* and other media that covered the games. We were also given the assignment of printing all the venue packets for the press.

It wasn't long before we realized that the skill sets necessary to run an independent business were the same ones we'd learned in our various management positions at the airlines. Sales, hiring, operations, and organizational skills had come into play without us even thinking about it.

We felt emboldened. We realized that we could realistically take on our first choice of the franchise world, which was owning a McDonald's restaurant.

We completed an application from McDonald's and sent it in with the hope of getting an interview. We later learned that thousands of applications were sent in every month. But since we had experience in the corporate world and as business owners, we were contacted and an interview was set up.

On the appointed day, we headed to the corporate offices of McDonald's on Wilshire Boulevard in Los Angeles. We didn't know quite what to expect but we had always done well in interviews and were good together, playing off each other. The corporate offices were as impressive as we had expected. We were shown into a conference room where we met with the franchising manager. We went over our backgrounds and why we wanted to become McDonald's franchisees.

As we described our experiences in management, our understanding of how to train and supervise employees, and our success in customer relations, the franchising manager explained how McDonald's training worked. We would first be put into a restaurant for what they called an OJE—on-the-job evaluation—over a three-day period. When the OJE was completed and if all had gone well, we would be brought back for another interview.

The franchise manager made it clear that the purpose of the OJE was not only to evaluate the applicant's desire and understanding of what it took to own a McDonald's restaurant. It was also to demonstrate that this was a full-time, hands-on business. In the training period that followed, we would be taught everything there is to know about running a McDonald's. Completing this training could take up to two or three years. We would do the training part time, putting in at least twenty hours a week. There would be no cost to us for the training, but we should not sell our home or quit our jobs in the expectation of becoming McDonald's franchisees. There was no guarantee that we would ultimately be awarded a store.

I inquired whether I could do the training full time. Since we owned our own business, Tina could manage that while I trained. The answer I got was a firm no. I then asked about opportunities for long-term growth. The answer came in the form of a question: "Do you know how many Black people would love to own even *one* McDonald's?" On that note we said, "Thank you, we hope to hear from you," and closed the interview. Sometimes you have to be strategically silent.

CHAPTER 8

"Billions and Billions Sold"

But remember the LORD your God. For it is he who gives you
the ability to produce wealth, and so confirms his covenant,
that which he swore to your ancestors, as it is today.

—DEUTERONOMY 8:18

The journey to success comes with revisits, rewards and repositions but never lose the reason that dared you to dream. McDonalds was America's great corporate success story of the 1960s. Years later, high-tech innovators like Microsoft and Apple seemed to create their own entirely new and original universe, but the McDonald's phenomenon happened differently. McDonald's did not "come out of nowhere." Instead, McDonald's was the culmination of some powerful preexisting societal trends. Simply put, McDonald's was an idea whose time had come.

We can look at McDonald's history through two separate but overlapping story lines. We can call the first of these narratives "the legend of McDonald's." It's certainly the better known of the two stories, though probably not the most insightful.

According to the legend, a fifty-two-year-old milkshake machine salesman named Ray Kroc got an order for eight machines from a restaurant in San Bernardino, California. The fact that a single restaurant was buying eight milkshake machines intrigued Kroc, and he traveled to San Bernardino to investigate.

There he found a drive-in hamburger restaurant with several key features. In contrast to drive-ins as they had existed since the 1930s, there were no waitresses—not even on roller skates—who came to customers' cars to take orders. There was no interior seating either. Customers exited their cars and placed orders at the restaurant's service window. The orders were picked up at that window also, and it all happened very quickly.

The menu was limited, and the items were inexpensive. Hamburgers, fries, and milk shakes were pretty much the extent of it.

There were a few other key elements, but this was basically what Ray Kroc encountered in San Bernardino. As the legend goes on to describe, when he saw the potential of the original McDonald's location, he decided to turn it into a franchise empire, and the rest is history.

The non-legend story of McDonald's may seem less dramatic, but it's more revealing about the real sources of the company's success. Once Ray Kroc struck a deal with the McDonald brothers of San Bernardino, his low-franchising fees allowed new restaurants to open rapidly. But the company's profits had remained stubbornly low.

What put McDonald's solidly on the right track was not production-line hamburgers sold at low prices. It was the company's real estate arm, called the Franchise Realty Corporation, which was created by a McDonald's executive named Harry Sonneborn.

To operate the Franchise Realty Corporation, Ray Kroc scouted locations for new stores, with a focus on cheap vacant land near highways. The Franchise Realty Corporation then bought or leased the land and then subleased it to franchisees at a substantial markup. McDonald's became the landlord of the franchisees, who paid the company either a fixed rate or a percentage of sales, whichever was greater. As sales and prices rose over time, therefore, McDonald's income from the subleases continued to rise. In the early days, Ray would award territories to people. Some were deals written on a paper napkin.

This was simply a continuation of the plantation economics and sharecropping economy that existed in America hundreds of years ago. In the context of McDonald's franchising, that has never really gone away. As an African American, I may be more sensitive to this than other people, but the truth is still the truth.

In the old South, a plantation economy relied on the sale and export of cash crops as a source of income. The larger a crop's harvest—and the smaller the cost of harvesting it—the more efficient and profitable the plantation became. In 1750, African slaves comprised 50 percent of the South's total population.

Today the plantation model that existed in 1750 is still the foundation of McDonald's, which is one of the world's largest land owners with over thirty thousand pieces of property. One important difference between eighteenth- and nineteenth-century plantations and McDonald's current version is that the workers and sharecroppers are of all races and ethnicities. I'm sure this is a positive development, but the underlying system is surprisingly unchanged.

McDonald's franchisees do not own the land upon which a restaurant sits, nor do they own the building itself. The rent they pay to the company is based on the sales of products—"crops"—which are primarily hamburgers. The franchisee must buy supplies exclusively from providers designated by the company. In the old days, these approved suppliers were called "the company store."

The operation of each McDonald's restaurant is monitored by a field service representative, who is analogous to a plantation's overseer or field boss. If a restaurant does not operate correctly or if it underperforms, a franchisee can be put on review and possibly lose their franchise.

The franchisee is responsible for maintaining the restaurant's building, plus whatever improvements the company requires or that may be required by municipal regulations. In addition, the franchisee is responsible for property taxes. Whenever value of the property rises due to improvements made by the franchisee, the property tax rises accordingly.

The company reaps the benefits of the property's increased value on their books, while the franchisee carries the debt on their portion of the costs, plus paying rent to McDonald's. There is little difference here from a sharecropper having to maintaining their own houses. McDonald's is the twentieth-century equivalent of the 1750 plantations and the franchisees are twenty-first-century sharecroppers.

This is the reality of how a vision in the mind of Ray Kroc in 1955 has turned into a company that is the largest and most recognized restaurant chain in the world. Kroc's dream has evolved into a Wall Street–driven company that has put profit before brand.

The profits derived from the company's nearly twenty-five hundred franchisees and thirty thousand employees hugely benefit the corporation and its shareholders. When the restaurants are profitable, the franchisees naturally benefit as well, but in a much less substantial way. A top manager who is terminated will receive a massive "golden parachute," while an underperforming franchisee will have little equity in the business after years of work and will sometimes even face bankruptcy. The company will sell the store to another individual who will maintain the money machine for the McDonald's plantation.

Along with the legend of Ray Kroc's assembly-line hamburgers and the importance of McDonald's leasing innovations, there were also large-scale sociological factors that worked in McDonald's interests. Earlier I mentioned the growth of air travel and the highway system as benefitting McDonald's. But the fact that people were traveling would have been less significant were it not for the national advertising campaigns that Ray Kroc began as McDonald's began to become profitable.

When a McDonald's billboard went up in Chicago, for example, it was more than just an advertisement for the stores in that city. It was an advertisement for McDonald's in general. It was an advertisement for every McDonald's restaurant at once, because every restaurant was the same as all the others.

If a family was driving from Oklahoma City to Albuquerque, they could pull off Interstate 40 in Amarillo and enter a McDonald's exactly like the one back home. They would not have to drive around in a strange city looking for a place to feed the kids. They would not even have to look at an unfamiliar menu. McDonald's menu was the same everywhere, and so was a McDonald's hamburger. A family could always rely on a clean bathroom with changing tables for infants.

Besides the hamburgers and the menus, there was another aspect of the company's sameness in the early days. McDonald's was by and for White people. This was not bigotry or intentional racism. It was just the way the business developed.

In a similar way, when the business eventually changed to connect with the African American market, it wasn't because there had been some shift in the moral sentiments of the ownership. It was a matter of economic opportunity, or even necessity.

This is how such things have happened in many areas of American life. When the University of Alabama began to include Black football players in the 1970s, the civil rights movement was not the reason. Martin Luther King Jr. had already come and gone and there were still no Black players on the Alabama team. The change came when Alabama suffered a very public defeat to the University of Southern California and Sam Cunningham, its Black ballcarrier.

There is even evidence that Paul Bryant, the Alabama coach, had deliberately scheduled the USC game to show the public why it was time to integrate the team. There may have been racist Alabama fans, but they would put that aside if it was causing losses on the field.

Before long, and well into the 1970s, you could observe the strange phenomenon of college football games with mostly Black players on the field and not a single Black person in the grandstands. This was a complex phenomenon that was a form of sharecropping. It was analogous to the operation of McDonald's and other business. It would become more complex as time passed, in the sense that Black athletes and entertainers were eventually making huge amounts of money. But strange as it might seem, the essential sharecropping structure would remain in place.

CHAPTER 9

INTO THE GOLDEN ARCHES

Opportunities don't happen, you create them.

—CRIES GROSSER

As Tina and I left the interview with the franchise manager, we were both quiet getting into our car. We were trying to digest how the interviewer felt about us, and we were also trying to figure out how we felt ourselves. As we came down from the adrenaline rush of this interview, both of us began to feel disappointed. First, there was the rather insulting response to my question about a possible future with McDonald's. But a bigger concern was the timeline of when we might be able to purchase a franchise.

We didn't know how long the opportunity to become franchisees would be there. How long would that door be open? During our research, we had also looked at Burger King. We knew some Burger King franchisees and had spent some time with them. We learned that the Burger King model, unlike that of McDonald's, puts most of the responsibility on the franchisee.

Burger King franchisees themselves select the site on which a store will be built. Although this can be empowering for the franchisees, it is also very labor intensive. As the process goes on, the sense of empowerment can also seem like a lack of corporate support. Then, once a location is selected, the major difference between Burger King and McDonald's emerges: The Burger King franchisee could be the owner of the land and the building, or they can be leased.

The franchisee must execute due diligence on the site in terms of demographics and zoning. Sometimes aerial photographs will be taken. The company does provide some assistance in these areas, but much of the cost is borne by the prospective franchisee. In contrast to McDonald's, at Burger King the number of stores we could own would be up to us, assuming we were financially qualified. In this sense, the potential for both short- and long-term growth was much greater.

We applied to Burger King and were invited for an interview. The interview went well, and I would begin my training at a Burger King on Jefferson Avenue, directly across the street from USC. Burger King's training lasted two weeks. After I completed the two weeks, Tina and I sat down and considered our options.

During my training I became aware of a corner site close to where we lived. It was occupied by a gas station that was going to close. I contacted Burger King's corporate office and suggested that they look at the site and possibly help me lease it. I should have known that McDonald's real estate team was aware of the site and the regional vice president (who would later become one of our best friends) had given the team a blank check to buy the site outright. This all happened before I could even get Burger King's attention. Based on this experience, I felt there was no way we were going to be able to compete with the number one fast-food franchise in the world.

This was a big problem. Tina and I sat down to figure out what we could do now, after already turning down McDonald's offer to begin training. Meanwhile, we still owned our printing franchise.

Once again, divine intervention stepped into our lives. I received a call from a dear friend of my mother, a woman named Rose, whom my mother had worked with at United Airlines. Rose moved on from United a few years earlier and was now the director of human resources at Disney.

It turned out that Rose had a friend who worked at Norman Lear Productions, one of the most powerful TV production companies in Hollywood. Through her friend, Rose learned that Lear was beginning development of a pilot for a new series and was looking for a Black couple to work as consultants. The pilot was called *Full House* and it had an all-Black cast.

Rose remembered that I had done some writing and had experience in the industry with Sugar Ray. With that in mind, she recommended Tina and I and we were invited to dinner with the producers of the pilot, who had done several hit shows in the past. They described *Full House* as a comedy about three generations of a Black family living in Chicago—grandparents, parents, and kids. The father was an airline pilot and his wife was a fashion designer.

At that time, there were few Black writers in Hollywood, and the writers on this show were White. Supposedly, Black writers couldn't be hired because they didn't have experience. But they couldn't get experience without ever being hired. Tina and I were not considered as writers, but at the end of the dinner we were offered employment as well-paid consultants. As Black people, we were supposed to provide "authenticity."

This seemed like a good opportunity for us, because we could do the work at Universal Studios without disrupting our printing business. On our first day, we arrived to meet the cast and read through a scene of the pilot.

This scene took place when the family was having dinner. The father and the grandfather were talking about their plans for going to a hockey game. I politely interrupted and mentioned that "the only thing Black at a hockey game in Chicago is the puck. Maybe they should go to a Bulls game instead." The producers agreed, and the script was changed.

A Black psychologist was also working on the show. Like us, he was hired to make sure that the show was culturally accurate. When we broke for lunch on the first day, we went to lunch with the psychologist and he inquired what we did for a living. We told him about the printing business, and we also described our experience with McDonald's. He said, "My good friend Reggie is with McDonald's, and he's coming for dinner on Tuesday. Why don't you come over and meet him?"

We accepted the invitation and had a good conversation over dinner with Reggie. When we described our interview at McDonald's, he listened intently. Then he said, "Look, give the new-franchising manager a call on Monday and set up another meeting."

I didn't know it at the time, but now I see this connection with Reggie as another occasion of divine intervention. He would become our close friend for the next thirty years and we remain close to this day. The Bible says, "Trust in the lord with all your heart and lean not on your own understanding: In all your ways acknowledge Him, and He will direct your path."

We called the McDonald's corporate offices and set up a meeting with the new-franchising manager. As we drove up to the building, I turned to Tina said, "When we get in the meeting, don't mess it up this time." I was kidding her, of course. Tina and I have always had a wonderful relationship. We can always make each other laugh in times of stress. It's worked for us for forty-four years and there's no reason to mess with success.

We sat in the conference room for the second time, with the franchising manager across the table from us with a file folder in front of him. By way of introduction, I said, "Mr. Webb suggested we request this interview for a further discussion of the applicant program."

"Right," said the manager. "When do you want to start?"

I was shocked that there was no resistance. "Well," I said, "I'd like to start as soon as possible"

"Great. Let's set a date."

We settled on the day after Labor Day, 1985. Then, just as I had in the first interview, I requested to do the program full time.

"No problem. Mr. Webb said that anything you want should be fine."

We had spent all of fifteen minutes in that conference room, and now we were on our way. Leaving the interview, we felt like we could see the future. We were sure there was a plan for us. We had seen doors close, only to find that others were opening. We would make this journey together, and we would make it by Faith.

Tina and I decided that we would both go through the training period, but we felt that I should go first while we kept the printing business to maintain our income. Our son Jeremy was now eight years old. His school was only a few minutes from Sir Speedy, so we could pick him up and he would do his homework at the shop until we went home.

My training location was at a McDonald's in Burbank, northwest of Los Angeles. The franchisee was nicknamed Frenchy, and we became good friends. By now I had left United for good and—even while working in the print shop during the day—I was able to put in almost forty hours a week at the McDonald's. I was there nights, weekends, and days when I could be out of the shop.

The training in Burbank consisted of practical experience plus study and classroom work with written tests. I had been away from United now for several years and had kept in touch with only a few friends. One day I heard someone call my name as I was working fries. When I turned, it was one of the sales reps whom I knew from United. His eyes were as big as saucers as he watched me. I said hello and kept working.

As he left, I noticed him hesitate just outside the door and look back at me. It struck me that he probably thought that I had reached rock bottom working at McDonald's. Because I was able to train full time, I was also able to attend McDonald's "Hamburger University" in Chicago in June of 1986. I have reminded myself many times that sometimes you have to just be still and listen. In all things He will direct your path.

CHAPTER 10

Pine Bluff?

*But they that wait upon the LORD shall renew their
strength; They shall mount up with wings as eagles;
They shall walk, and not faint.*

—ISAIAH 40:31

Thirteen years before any of this, my mother had been diagnosed
with breast cancer. Since then, the cancer had been in remis-
sion, but Tina called the day before my graduation from Hamburger
University and told me that the disease had returned.

My mother had gone into a hospital in Indianapolis, where she
now lived. I flew to Indianapolis, and when I walked into my mom's
hospital room I was happy to see how surprised and glad she was.
But she had lost a shocking amount of weight. It scared me, but I
didn't let on that I was concerned. And anyway, my mother's spirits
were lifted by having me there and she was able to go home the day
after I arrived.

Being out of the hospital made her feel much better. Aside from
the weight loss, she felt alert and able to do anything mentally, but

*Betty Lewis-Golder,
Harold's mother*

she just didn't have the strength to get up and go. I knew, however, that she had recurrent cancer. It had metastasized through her body, so that any treatments available at that time would have been useless. I believe the protocols available today for treating her type of cancer could have saved her life.

I stayed in Indianapolis as long as I could. Shortly after I returned home, a call came from the franchising manager asking us to meet him the following week at the next applicants' meeting. We felt this was a good sign. There was probably some sort of opportunity he wanted to present to us. No one in McDonald's knew about my mother's illness.

After the applicants' meeting, we went to have coffee with Randy, the manager. Yes, there was something he wanted us to consider. That was the good news. The less than good news was that the opportunity was not in California, Texas, or Arizona. Those were the states for which we had indicated interest, since there were no possibilities in Los Angeles.

"You don't necessarily get a location right where you want," Randy said. Then he added, "But knowing that Tina is from Louisiana, I want to let you know that there's an opportunity for a new store being built in Pine Bluff, Arkansas."

As Tina dug her fingernails into my leg, we kept our composure and said that we would definitely consider this possibility. We left the meeting and immediately started trying to figure out how to diplomatically turn down this offer. Our corporate experience told us that you can't just blurt it out when something doesn't sit well with you. If you want people to concur with your decisions, you have to make them feel like they made those decisions themselves.

The next day I conferred with Frenchy, the McDonald's franchisee who had trained me at his restaurant in Burbank. I told him about the Pine Bluff offer and said that we didn't want to go to Pine Bluff. Frenchy replied that sometimes an offer like that is intended as a test to see what your reaction will be. He said there might be another offer behind this one.

Frenchy told us to do some homework and return with a good reason for not wanting to go to Pine Bluff.

Frenchy had been involved with McDonald's for many years both on the corporate side and as a franchisee. He was well versed on how they operated. We later learned that the Pine Bluff offer had been made to several applicants and that the response was sometimes less that professional. Some of those applicants were never awarded a restaurant.

Tina and I went to the library—there was no Google in those days—and studied the Pine Bluff area. We quickly noticed that this was an agricultural community. We also noticed the average temperature in the summer was very hot, as is sometimes the case in river towns.

That was enough for us. I waited a few days, and then called Randy. I said we had given this some real consideration and we were grateful for the opportunity. But our son was eight years old and we weren't comfortable with him growing up in an agricultural community. We wanted him to go to school in a more metropolitan area.

As Frenchy had predicted, Randy responded that this wasn't a problem. Now he wanted us to go to San Diego to meet with the regional vice president for that area. At that time, the regional vice presidents decided who would be awarded restaurants in their markets. Franchising managers such as John recommended qualified applicants to the regional vice presidents.

Randy explained that for the moment there wasn't any opportunity in San Diego, but he wanted us to meet the regional manager in case something came up soon.

As we drove to San Diego on the appointed day, Tina proclaimed to me that there was, in fact, an opportunity for a restaurant in San Diego. I reminded her, however, that we had been told there were no opportunities in San Diego, or anywhere else in California. But her "mother's intuition" was working.

At the corporate offices in San Diego, we discussed with the regional vice president our background and experience, and we described how we saw ourselves running a McDonald's restaurant. The regional vice president then asked if we knew the specific purpose of this meeting. We replied, as Randy had told us, that the meeting was to get acquainted in case an opportunity opened in San Diego.

We were then informed that there was, in fact, an opportunity in San Diego. The regional vice president asked us to drive by the location to see what we thought. He also said that the location was in a "rough area," by which he meant the mostly Black community in the southern part of the city.

We agreed to drive by the location, as he suggested. In the car, I also complimented Tina on her accurate prediction about a restaurant being available. We drove to the address we had been given, but we weren't sure we had gone to the right place. Yes, there was an empty lot suitable for a McDonald's. But wasn't it supposed to be in a rough area?

After checking the address once again, we looked at each other and laughed. We lived in Los Angeles and I had grown up in a much rougher area than what we saw here. In our estimation, this was by no means rough.

We later discovered why the company was concerned. A McDonald's had been built less than a mile from the new proposed location. On the opening night, a gang member was shot and killed there. The restaurant was closed shortly after the shooting. Ten years had passed since that incident, but the company remained uncertain about the area.

Before we even got back to Los Angeles, we called the regional vice president. I said "We drove by the location and we understand that you had concerns about the area. But we feel we could handle it and we'd like to give it a shot."

We were awarded the restaurant. We thought that we wanted the site we found in Los Angeles with Burger King. We had prayed on that site, and the Lord said no. Sometimes He says no because it's not His plan for you.

CHAPTER 11

END AND BEGINNING

The only way to do great work is to love what you do.
If you haven't found it yet, keep looking. Don't settle.

—STEVE JOBS

This was all happening in July, when the company had begun preconstruction work on the restaurant building. When a site is purchased or leased, McDonald's decides whether they will own and run the restaurant or franchise it. In our case, because the company had made a late decision to franchise, our lead time was short.

Once a contractor is hired to build a restaurant, a time line is set with an opening date for the business. There is little margin for error or delays. Our groundbreaking date was set for September, so we had to move quickly. This was going to involve radical changes in every area of our lives.

The first step was to get back to Los Angeles, sell our home, and liquidate everything. We had already put our printing business on the market and we had gotten an offer. We wanted to avoid having to get a loan for a down payment if McDonald's came up with an

Grand opening of the first McDonald's

opportunity—which they now had done. We didn't want to miss an opportunity just because we didn't have money for the down payment. And while all this was going on, we also listed our home for sale.

Tina and I took turns going to Indianapolis to help my mother, whose cancer was continuing to spread. She had to take medication every four hours for the pain. Despite everything she was going through, somehow, she was still able to share in the planning of our restaurant.

Tina was handling the décor of our restaurant, which is the responsibility of the franchisee. She was able to share the design and colors for the restaurant with my mother. But by late August my mother was in and out of the hospital. Her bones had become so brittle that on one visit her leg broke when she was being helped onto an examining table. When she was at home after a surgery, she needed medication every two hours.

This was all just a terrible and overwhelming experience for everyone. This should have been a high point in our lives, but it was the lowest point. Life can be like that, yet we had to persevere. Our faith tells us that God won't give us any more than we can handle. We believed that with all our hearts. We had to trust that He knew our limits better than we did.

My mother and Tina were very close. Despite her cancer, my mom did everything she could to help Tina keep me together. She knew how worried and broken we were, knowing that there was nothing we or anyone could do to really help. On one of Tina's visits, my mother told her, "Don't let anything that happens to me interfere with what you have to do." I knew she was very happy that we were going to own a McDonald's—to be financially secure and able to provide for Jeremy's future. I also knew she was very glad that Tina was my wife. She knew that I had found my perfect mate, and that I was going to be okay.

As we approached the September groundbreaking date for the restaurant in San Diego, my mother's cancer was getting progressively worse. Bishop Golder, my stepfather, called me in California and told me that I should come to Indianapolis right away. When I arrived at the hospital, my mother was so sedated that she could barely speak. But I was very glad that she was at least able to acknowledge that I was there.

She passed a few days later, on September 21, 1986, which was her birthday. She was sixty-one. I will always believe she found her peace knowing that Tina and I would be all right. She could let go and relieve herself of the pain. I left the hospital so allayed that her suffering was over. I also felt intense guilt. I was torn between wanting her to be relieved of the pain and wanting to hold on to her. It tears your insides out to see a loved one suffer and not be able to do anything to help.

I called Tina and asked her to come with Jeremy to Indianapolis. When she asked how Mom was doing, I said it wasn't good. Although I didn't tell Tina my mom had died, I sensed that she knew. I told her that I was at the house, and she knew that I would not have left the hospital if my mother was still alive.

When I met Tina's plane at the airport, there was a moment, while waiting for the luggage, to take Jeremy outside. Telling him that his grandmother had passed was one of the most difficult things I've ever had to do. My own feeling of hurt was compounded by the pain Jeremy was feeling at the age of eight. He had always looked forward to the times he'd come to Indianapolis to spend a week or two with his grandmother. He loved her so much and she worshipped him.

We began planning my mother's funeral in Indianapolis, as well as taking her back to Los Angeles for a funeral there as well. She had spent most of her life in Los Angeles and wanted to be buried there. My mother was always very organized. As we went through some written requests she had left us, we realized that she had carefully planned out her entire funeral service. We, of course, followed her instructions and arranged everything exactly as she had wanted. In 1984, when she planned her service three years before her passing, she had written this poem to be included in the program:

> *GREAT GAIN*
> *When I lie in sweet repose*
> *do not weep for me;*
> *For when we leave this mortal frame*
> *'tis only then I'm really free.*
> *At my grave, do not cry,*
> *'tis an empty house beneath the*
> *sod. My spirit did not die*
> *I have gone to be with god*
> *for there is a better place*
> *And to be absent from this body,*
> *is to see him face to face.*

Would you have me still abide here
in a body filled with pain?
Or dwell with him who died for me?
This alone is great gain!!!!
Betty Golder
September 15, 1984

We remained on a timetable for the construction of the restaurant. We had the funeral in Indianapolis and the funeral in Los Angeles a week later. The very next day we had to be in San Diego for the groundbreaking. We were still at two extremes of an emotional spectrum. Tina helped me close the escrow on the printing business, and she worked two jobs so that we didn't go through the money we needed for the McDonald's. We accepted an offer on our home in Los Angeles and began looking for a rental house in San Diego.

Then a real problem arose. On our way to San Diego to sign the contracts with McDonald's, I got a call from my uncle that the offer on our house had fallen out of escrow. Now I had a decision to make. Should I let the company know that our house had fallen out of escrow? Or should we move forward signing the contracts and have faith that things would work out?

We signed the contracts with McDonald's. We also began looking for a house to rent and a school for Jeremy. When we returned from San Diego, I got a call from my aunt who was handling the sale of the house. She reminded me that a person had looked at the house before taking a vacation out of the country for some time. Now he was back, and she had let him know that the house had fallen out of escrow. He immediately made an offer. We accepted the offer and the house went back into escrow.

While the escrow moved forward, we found a house to rent in San Diego and began the move. The restaurant was in the early stages of construction and we were not needed on site. The time line seemed to be moving in our favor. Jeremy was in his new school in time for the start of classes, we were situated in our house, and the restaurant would open on February 9, 1987. We began introducing ourselves to the community and we met with officials in city hall.

We also "adopted" the local high school, Lincoln High, and began interviewing prospective employees among the students. During our visit to Lincoln, we learned that the school's funding was severely limited. In a minority area with low-income families, there wasn't much outside support. We were glad that our business would bring jobs and an attractive restaurant into the community, and we wanted to bring whatever else we possibly could.

In Lincoln's auto repair classroom, I discovered that the whole auto repair curriculum was from a textbook. There was no practical training because they there was no car to train on. When we moved to San Diego, my car was a 1972 Datsun 280Z with one hundred twenty thousand miles. I was able to buy myself another car after opening our restaurant, so I donated my Datsun to the automobile department at Lincoln High.

CHAPTER 12

MINDING THE STORE

There is no passion to be found playing small—
in settling for a life that is less than the one you are
capable of living.

—NELSON MANDELA

We got very little sleep during the nights before our restaurant officially opened. We were working intently on last-minute preparations. The ribbon-cutting ceremony took place on February 9, 1987, complete with family, friends, local politicians cooking hamburgers, and another emotional coincidence. My father had died when I was seven years old, and I never knew his birthdate. In fact, it was only a few years ago that I found his birth certificate while going through some family papers and realized that we had opened the restaurant on his birthday. I like to think that this validated our work as a continuation of the hard work to which my dad had devoted his life. He was determined to do his best for the family and I felt the same way. All these years later, I felt that I had spiritually reconnected with my father.

Groundbreaking first McDonald's

At the ribbon-cutting celebration we had pastries set out for the dignitaries and other guests. Carl Hargrave, the other Black franchisee in San Diego, had been mentoring us since our arrival in town. He took me aside and said, "Look, you're not here to serve free baked goods. Put the Danish away, open the doors, and start selling hamburgers." With Carl's advice, we did just that and the restaurant was immediately jammed. We learned an important point: be fully prepared when you open a McDonald's. Customers don't care if it's your first day or not. They're looking for the same excellent customer experience that they have become accustomed to.

In addition to Carl and Alma, his wife, several of our Black franchisee friends came to San Diego to help us at our opening. They cooked food, served customers, and made sure all systems were working well. This was hugely helpful.

Tina and I were so exhausted on that first day, and throughout that first week, that we can't even remember it.

Our first year was a success and we were able to explore buying a home in San Diego rather than continuing to rent. If we didn't buy a home, we would have a big tax liability from the sale of our house in Los Angeles. This issue was the first time we bumped heads with McDonald's. I got a call from a staff accountant asking me why I had refinanced my loan with the bank. This was an example of the company's total oversight and control. McDonald's had banks reporting to them on something as personal as a refinance to buy a home.

I explained to the accountant that we were facing a capital gains tax on the home we sold. I would have to pay taxes on the proceeds if I didn't purchase another home. I pointed out that the money would have to be spent one way or another, and purchasing a home was the best option.

The firm tone of my response was obviously not what the accountant was used to. There has long been a feeling by some corporate employees at McDonald's that a franchisee works for the corporation and must be subservient to corporate staff. I soon got a call from the regional vice president. He wanted to know what I said to the accountant that had brought her to tears. I explained that I had been surprised by the nature of the call, but that I had gone ahead and explained the reason for my refinancing. He said that he understood and agreed, but also asked me to be more understanding. I too agreed, but also asked him to help his staff be more tactful when they needed information. I didn't deserve to feel like I was being interrogated.

At that point, we had been part of the McDonald's system for about a year. This was the first of many lessons leading us to a realization that the "family" company Ray Kroc founded was evolving into a Wall Street–driven corporate behemoth.

Meanwhile, we had been embraced by the San Diego community and we were rewarded in many ways for our efforts in the city. We were the providers of first jobs for many young people in the area. A significant number of them came from broken homes in tough neighborhoods, with no positive role models. Over the coming years, we would see our employees buy their first cars and first homes and graduate from high school and college.

But even when we felt we were protecting the young people, they also felt like they were protecting us. There was one big strong kid named Frank who liked to stand behind me, as if he were a bodyguard. He always had my back. Working at McDonald's allowed him to get his first car. He also used to talk to me about his relationship with his father.

Kids would come into the store even after their shift was finished. I remember asking one kid, "Why are you still here?" and he said, "My mother's boyfriend kicked me out. I don't have anywhere else to go." Tina had one girl come to her and tell her that she'd been raped.

Our first restaurant was successful right from the opening. It was the best thing that had appeared for that part of San Diego for quite some time.

The first few nights there was a group of guys hanging out in the parking lot. They were gang members. There was a bunch of trash lying around. I went out and said, "I appreciate your coming to the store and helping us to make it successful. We've put a lot of work and money into this. The thing is, when you hang out in the parking lot it can seem intimidating to customers. I just want to be upfront about that, so do me a favor and put your trash in the trash bin and don't hang out too long."

They agreed, and there was never a problem after that. Bloods and Crips gang members patronized the restaurant and worked side by side. Our McDonald's became a neutral zone. It had also become something very different from what the company had been at its beginning.

When McDonald's was founded in 1955, it was a White male enterprise until Herman Petty became the first African American franchisee, purchasing his first restaurant on the South Side of Chicago in 1968. Going forward, African American franchisees purchased stores in Harlem, Los Angeles, Detroit, and elsewhere, but always in the African American communities of those cities.

In 1972, the National Black McDonald's Operator's Association (NBMOA) was formed by the few African American franchisees who existed at the time. The main purpose was to form a self-help and advocacy organization that would support the interests of African American operators on issues they were facing with the company. Some of those early issues included an absence of field support and a lack of understanding of the Black communities.

For example, Lee Dunham, one of the pioneering African American franchisees, told me that for the first year after he opened his store in Harlem, he slept in the basement of his store and worked seven days a week to build his business. During that first year, he never met a single representative from McDonald's until one day Ray Kroc came into his store. Ray, upon seeing the struggle Lee was having in the operation, asked what kind of help Lee had received from the company. When Lee stated that he had not seen anyone at all from McDonald's, Ray Kroc was furious.

Ray, Lee said, stood on a chair in the restaurant and apologized to the customers for the store not running like it should. Ray then called the corporate office and demanded the field service rep get out to the store and give Lee the assistance he needed and deserved in order to bring the store up to what it should be. For the rest of his career, Lee would continue to be one of the best franchisees in the system, and one of the presidents of the NBMOA. He was also the first African American to open a McDonald's on Wall Street.

By 1988, as we entered our second year as franchisees, the NBMOA was focused on the gap between the African American franchisees and their White counterparts. The time had long passed when we should be thought of as only being able to build stores in the African American communities. We deserved equal opportunity to grow in any community and all communities. But there was still resistance on the part of the company, as well as from some White franchisees who saw Black ownership as a threat to their growth.

There was no trouble as long as Black franchisees operated only in Black communities. But African American owners feeling entitled to expand into any neighborhood was not a welcomed thought by many in the McDonald's universe. Yet by this time, we were well into the 1980s, when the gains of the civil rights movement twenty years earlier had become established in American life. African American communities were the most loyal customers of McDonald's, and the African American presence in the company should not and could not be taken for granted.

The value of commitment to the inner city by the African American operators in the form of jobs and giving back to their communities dramatically revealed itself in 1992. Riots broke out following the acquittal of the Los Angeles police officers who arrested and beat Rodney King. One magazine wrote about the smoke clearing in and around Los Angeles, with hundreds of businesses burned to the ground. But rising from the ashes, standing tall and undamaged, was a McDonald's restaurant. It was a testament to the many years of commitment to the communities by the African American operators.

From the time we moved to San Diego, we began building our ties in the community, as well as introducing ourselves to the political power brokers in the city. We made the rounds at city hall, introducing ourselves to everyone from the mayor to the city councilmen. Our goal was to let them know that we were building a McDonald's in the community that would not only serve food but would provide jobs and give back to the community.

This isn't how most people think of McDonald's. As time passed, we had former employees come to see us, and now they were doctors and lawyers. We always asked them to give something back, so they would speak to the kids who were working for us now. It was really a beautiful thing.

We tailored the restaurant to the community. We had African American art on the walls, and Tina had a great idea to put grits on the menu.

We also started scholarship programs that worked out well. When an employee applied for a scholarship, we asked them to write a letter describing the circumstances of their lives and why they wanted a scholarship. We had a committee that reviewed those letters, and sometimes there wasn't a dry eye in the room. There was one kid from Africa who described walking across the desert to come to America. He had lost his family. It was powerful message, and there were lots of letters like that.

During the next twenty years we were never robbed. Across the street from us, the Jack in the Box and the Taco Bell restaurants were robbed on several occasions. One morning we got call from the Jack in the Box alerting us that they had been robbed, with a description of the robbers and their car. I brought our team together, passed on the information, and told everyone to be on alert. As soon as I finished, our maintenance man who had been working outside that morning told us that the men had been in our restaurant that morning. They ordered breakfast, but they didn't rob us. Was it a coincidence that, years later when we sold the restaurant, it was robbed within a week?

CHAPTER 13

RESTAURANT FOR SALE

But he said to me, "My grace is sufficient for you, for
my power is made perfect in weakness." Therefore,
I will boast more gladly about my weakness, so that
Christ's power may rest on me. That is why, for Christ's
sake, I delight in weakness, in insults, in hardships,
in persecutions, in difficulties. For when I am weak,
then I am strong.

—2 CORINTHIANS 12-9-10

Ray Kroc had built his company on a model that he called the "three-legged stool." The three legs were the corporation, the suppliers, and the franchisees. Within that model, the corporation would need to be sure that the suppliers remained in business, otherwise the whole enterprise could not survive. To make this happen, our food suppliers were paid their costs plus 10 percent while the corporation received money from our rent and other service fees.

Our challenge as franchisees was to come up with a profit at the end of this food chain. In doing this, we discovered over time that the three-legged stool was more like two legs and a stump. We were the stump. It would become apparent to us over our thirty years with the company that the three-legged stool was not an accurate metaphor for what we were encountering. Instead, we had bought into a model that dated back to the Colonial days. We were sharecroppers. We did well, of course, and I don't mean to literally compare our lives to people who lived on plantations. But the sharecropper analogy does accurately describe the relationships that were in play.

Despite all that's been written about McDonald's in the decades since it started, most people don't understand that McDonald's is not primarily in the hamburger business. McDonald's is first and foremost in the real estate business. McDonald's owns more commercial real estate than any other company in America. Money is made from leasing the land to the franchisees. McDonald's is a land-investment company disguised in a Ronald McDonald costume.

When we had been in our San Diego restaurant for almost a year, the company was preparing to award a new restaurant, which would be built about a mile from our present location. We naturally thought that we would be awarded that restaurant. However, we were told we weren't eligible because we hadn't been in the system for twelve months. This turned out to be a new rule.

We had fulfilled the company's desire for a restaurant in the Black community, and we had also satisfied the community's need for the restaurant. Now, going forward, we would have to fight for opportunities to grow. Two years went by. Then we learned that a new site was going to be developed in eastern San Diego County. It was a good distance from our restaurant but was not in a location where any other franchisee would be impacted.

When McDonald's develops a new site that's close to a franchisee's currently operating restaurant, the new site would go to that franchisee provided the franchisee is operationally and financially eligible. In this case, because there was no restaurant nearby, we asked to be considered for the site. We were initially turned down because the site was going to the company's joint venture partner.

By now I had more experience in dealing with the McDonald's bureaucracy. I fought for the site, and ultimately, I was successful. One day, while the restaurant was being built, I drove past the site. It was on a two-lane road in a recently developed shopping center. As I was about to turn into the lot, I found that a new median strip had been laid that would prevent drivers from making a left turn into the restaurant. To access the site, I had to drive another quarter of a mile to the next traffic light and make a U-turn. What's more, there was Jack in the Box right there on the corner by the traffic light.

The greatest challenge to growth as a McDonald's franchisee is opening a second restaurant. Franchisees double their operations, but they can't afford to double their management, so the franchisees must double their own responsibilities. Unwelcome surprises like the median strip don't make it any easier.

The McDonald's real estate rep had missed the notification about the median strip when he looked at the city plans. He was subsequently fired but now the damage was done. When the restaurant opened, sales were greatly affected by the median strip. In the first year, our sales were only half of what was projected. This was even though Tina had put together a comprehensive marketing plan and we had executed everything in it. This included an Easter egg hunt, pony rides, giveaways, a Ronald McDonald show, print ads, flyers, and mailers.

It became clear very quickly that the store was going to be a drain on our first restaurant. It was an automatic move for the company to dispatch the real estate department and field services out to determine the root cause of the drastic underperformance of the site. Over the next ninety days, we had visits from almost everyone in

McDonald's but Ray Kroc himself. They all looked in, around, on top, and underneath the restaurant to find something that we hadn't done that could contribute to the lack of sales.

Although the reason for the sales shortfall was obvious to me, the regional and corporate offices were looking for any answer that would vindicate them. When the zone vice president from corporate visited the new location, we went through the oversight of the median issue. Tina and I explained that we were having to subsidize losses from the second restaurant with revenue from the first restaurant. This would soon put us out of business.

We then drove back to our original restaurant where we were joined by Ray Aston, the corporate field service manager. The regional vice president glibly told us, "Well, some franchisees have had to sell their homes or liquidate their insurance policies to stay in the system. You'll just have to do whatever it takes."

At that time, we didn't know Ray Aston very well, but he would become a lifelong friend. When Ray saw me start to move from my seat, he put his hand on my shoulder to force me back down. He knew nothing good would come from me going across the table.

I attempted to calm down, but calming down was not made any easier by the fact that this zone vice president was African American. However, he had long since lost his identity and had learned to ignore the issues that African Americans face when trying to build a business. He had completely assimilated into the White environment of McDonald's and the corporate world in general. Unfortunately, we had no choice but to continue our appeal for help with this second restaurant that was threatening to put us out of business. We had put so much into this enterprise and we wanted to make it work.

We asked for a rent reduction to give us a chance to build up sales. He replied that the company did not lower rents in a situation like this. He added that McDonald's would look for another applicant or current franchisee who might want to take the restaurant. He didn't know how long that might take.

When I made it clear that we would shortly be out of money to cover both restaurants., he agreed to loan us one hundred fifty thousand dollars to hold us over until a buyer could be found. Once a buyer was found, he said the loan would be forgiven.

Months went by and we heard nothing about finding a buyer. This happened to be a year in which McDonald's held its national convention in Las Vegas. Tina and I attended, and we planned on meeting with Gerry Newman, the corporation's chief financial officer. He was a member of Ray Kroc's original inner circle. He was a genius with numbers and, more importantly for us, he was a friend and ally of the African American franchisees. He was aware of the unlevel corporate playing field, and he was truly an advocate for changing that.

At national conventions, Gerry Newman was like Don Corleone in the opening scenes of *The Godfather*. He held court in his hotel suite and dispensed justice to people who came to him with grievances. His rulings were informally known as "Newman Deals." Since Tina and I knew Gerry, it was easy for us to get an audience with him.

Our meeting with Gerry also included Bob Beavers, the zone vice president who had arranged the hundred fifty-thousand-dollar loan. Gerry took about five minutes to look at our profit-and-loss statements and the marketing plan that Tina had implemented. Then he told us "There's no way to make this work. It's going to put you out of business."

He turned to the zone vice president and said, "Why are they still in this restaurant?"

The vice president replied, "Well, we haven't found a buyer yet"

"That's not acceptable," Gerry said. "The company will buy the store. We can handle the losses."

That was great to hear. But then something very disturbing happened. When I asked the vice president about the loan, he denied his assurance that the loan would be forgiven. We were so grateful to Gerry and we didn't want the loan to become a distraction, so we did not challenge the vice president and let it go. We later refinanced the loan with a bank whose interest rate was lower than McDonald's.

Eventually the restaurant that was causing us so much trouble was sold to an applicant who had it for only a short time. Then it was sold to another franchisee in our market, and the rent was lowered to exactly what we had asked for. The fact is, the company can do whatever it wants, if it really wants to.

CHAPTER 14

Not All in the Family

When you get into a tight place and everything goes
against you till it seems that you cannot hold on for a
minute longer, never give up then, for that is just the
place and time when the tide will turn.

—HARRIET BEECHER STOWE

From the beginning of our careers with McDonald's, the theme of "family" had been proclaimed in every meeting and convention as a rallying cry to energize the franchisees to charge back out and move more product. It was almost as if they had hypnotized us, like a coach stirring up his football team to storm out of the locker room, or like a gladiator heading into the Coliseum in Rome ready to give it all to please the gods.

When you're part of such an organization, it's easy to buy into the idea that you are part of something bigger than yourself, and maybe better than yourself. You must live up to this opportunity. If you don't see it that way, there must be something wrong with you. You can never let anyone think you don't get it.

Being part of McDonald's was like being in the movie industry, or part of Disney. The company has so much influence and worldwide recognition that the name alone sparks interest in anyone you encounter. Tina and I consistently found ourselves treated like celebrities because we were McDonald's owners.

The feeling of belonging to something that big can consume you with a sense of pride, especially at the start of your career. Just imagine being a new franchisee and attending your first convention. You arrive in a location like Las Vegas or Florida with ten thousand other franchisees from one hundred twenty countries. The whole area has become "McDonald's Land," with welcoming billboards throughout the area and hotels whose rooms have been totally blocked for the convention.

The coordination and organization to take over a city takes a year of planning. Every activity is timed to the minute. There are camps and excursions for the franchisees' children, with full security. Transportation from the airport to the hotels runs twenty-four hours a day.

The convention center itself is converted to a sea of orange and yellow, McDonald's colors. Displays and vendor booths present innovations in banking, accounting, new uniforms, McDonald's art and jewelry, lobby décor displays, and playland equipment. Throughout the convention center there are multiple restaurants serving McDonald's food along with the newest items being tested around the world.

The franchisees are given the opportunity to meet and take pictures with Olympic athletes, race car drivers, and other celebrities who promote the company in print and TV.

One year, the company paid for the Barnum & Bailey Circus to do an entire private circus for the families in the convention hall. This was the first time in the circus's history anything like that had been done.

When the convention was held in Florida, the last two nights had the company buying out Disney World exclusively for McDonald's franchisees. As the busses rolled into the parking lots, the theme park had been converted to welcome the company. The flowers beside the pavement that led up to the main gates had been replanted with yellow arches of daffodils.

The park was open only to the franchisees, with unlimited access to everything from six in the evening until midnight. This was in addition to unlimited passes for children during the week. The final night would include a concert with an A-list celebrity.

Whatever concerns you might have had about the company, McDonald's plan was to make you feel that all was well. For the most part, the plan worked. There was no way you could leave the convention and not feel that you were part of something bigger than yourself, and that if you just hung in there everything would work itself out.

At one point there was a change in McDonald's regional management and a new regional vice president was appointed in our market. Don Thompson was African American and very much on a fast track with the company. We had first met briefly at a conference. He was personable, smart, and committed to engagement and partnership with the owners. He quickly gained their respect.

When one of the owners died, we received a call from Don. That owner, Lloyd, had been an original franchisee in the San Diego market, and he had one of the market's highest-volume restaurants. He also had two restaurants within a mile of our own first restaurant, one on either side of us. They were close enough so that our trading areas and our hiring overlapped.

Don discovered that taking over the position of vice president could be difficult. He had to handle any unfinished business as well as new issues, which in this case involved the disposition of Lloyd's restaurants.

I received a call from Don asking for some help and understanding. The previous vice president had promised Lloyd's restaurants to another owner in the market. McDonald's had a long-standing rule that when a company officer made a commitment, the company would honor it, even if it was the wrong decision and meant a loss to the company.

Unfortunately, that rule had not held true for us when the zone manager reneged on the loan he'd made to us when we had to sell our second restaurant. In any case, Don informed me that Lloyd's restaurants would not come to us because of the previous vice president's decision. Even though, geographically, the restaurants should have gone to us, we would be passed over once again.

I knew this was not easy for Don and I told him I would not challenge him. I could have, but I did not want the first questioning of his authority to come from me. Our friendship with Don and our support for him became very strong. I had a firm conviction to refrain from making an African American's job more difficult—especially considering my spiritual belief that everything happens for a reason. It's possible that this belief hurt our career at McDonald's. Perhaps we were too passive. But we were true to our faith.

By 2007, we had been operating three restaurants in the San Diego airports. As the costs of reinvestment and frequent changes in the look of the restaurants kept increasing, profits were decreasing. Other changes included experimenting with new menu items like the McLean, a shot at a healthier hamburger, which was a huge failure. Attempts at staging the lines in the lobby also didn't work.

We chose to sell our airport restaurants and position ourselves for growth by preserving some capital. When we made the deal on the sale, the general manager went to Don and challenged the price we were asking. Don responded that if the price worked for the person buying the restaurants, there was nothing to talk about. The general manager's underlying concern was our getting money out of the deal. It was a mind-set that couldn't accept African American owners doing as well as the White owners. Very unfair, but very true.

Around this time the company had been in some joint venture partnerships with owners of multiple franchises across the country. McDonald's would bundle as many as twelve of their restaurants together with the franchisee's restaurants. The franchisee would operate all the restaurants and would receive a management fee from the company. The profits would be split.

In our market, one of these partnerships soured. The franchisee and the company went into litigation. As the litigation moved forward, the franchisee's children were in the second-generation program to eventually own restaurants. But the general manager was trying to disqualify the children from the second-generation program.

I received a call from the son asking me, given my friendship with Don, if I could do anything to keep them in the program and purchase stores. But while the two parties were in litigation, there was nothing Don could do. I called Reggie, who was respected by both the company and owners. He was able to solve the problem.

Once a resolution was in place between the franchisee and the company, owners in our market were advised that the restaurants would be sold. Anyone with an interest in purchasing them should submit a written request, referencing the specific restaurants of interest.

Don asked me if there were any stores that I was interested in. I told him that I'd work with the list so there couldn't be any hint of favoritism.

We looked at the list and made our request to purchase a restaurant on the same street as one of our existing stores. But some substantial reinvestments would be required if that restaurant was purchased.

After looking at the list of reinvestments, it was clear that the joint venture partnership was not required to meet standards that would be expected of us. In a situation like this, where a franchisee sells a restaurant that does not meet minimum standards, the cost of all necessary corrections comes off the sale price.

We received a call from the general manager who advised us that if we wanted to purchase the restaurant, we had to purchase a Walmart McDonald's and a mall store as well. The Walmart cash flow was less than the required reinvestment, and the mall restaurant had a financial requirement that was also more than the cash flow. Additionally, there were only six months left on the restaurant's contract with the mall.

Confronted with all this, we chose to pass. I even believe that putting the added restaurants in the deal was an effort to get us to pass. But there were important revelations—along with frustration and disappointment—that would come to us after all the joint partnership stores were sold.

We had been told that everyone would have an opportunity to look at all the restaurants that had been in the partnership. A list of those restaurants was made available. But after the sales were finalized and the new ownerships were announced store by store, we discovered that not all the restaurants had been on the list. For example, the restaurant that we were not awarded the year after we became franchisees—which was a mile and a half from our original restaurant—had been left off the list. Outside the announced deal, it was sold to the former regional vice president, who had become a franchisee only recently.

Once again, there were different rules for different people. A good-old-boy side deal with the former regional vice president would cause us, the only African American owners in San Diego, to be excluded from an important opportunity. It was as simple as that.

The day after this revelation, I was parking my car at home when I saw Don drive by. At that time, we were living only a few blocks from each other. Don saw me and pulled up to our house. I shared with him my frustration at what had transpired. We were coming very close to getting out of McDonald's altogether. We had been passed over one too many times. But I also knew that leaving the system would only hurt our kids and erase our dream that they would be able to continue our legacy and become franchisees.

A short time later, we were invited to dinner by Don and his wife, Liz. There, Don told us that he had gotten a promotion and would be moving to Chicago. This was not a surprise, as we knew he was on a fast track with the company. His new title would be chief operating officer. This was a well-deserved promotion. We were very happy for him, and proud as well. Although we would not be in the same region as Don, we would continue working together on projects at the corporate level.

During twenty years in San Diego, we encountered every possible excuse McDonald's could come up with to keep us from getting new restaurants. For example, we could be told that a new location was too far from our existing restaurant. But then the award would go to another franchisee whose location was just as far as ours and sometimes farther.

Sometimes McDonald's would decide to sell a company-operated restaurant to a franchisee. These were not the best opportunities. They were typically old restaurants that needed lots of repair and reinvestment. Nevertheless, our next growth opportunity was for one of these company stores. By this time, the company was opening new restaurants around the world practically every day. All McDonald's restaurants are numbered in the order in which they were built. The new restaurants were numbered in the twenty thousands. We were sold number 1,039. It was about twenty years old.

The location was in San Diego's highest-crime area, which also included a large homeless population. The physical building was poorly lit and still had the original interior from when it was built in 1968. When a McDonald's restaurant is sold, there is always a walk-through of the property with the company rep. This includes taking an inventory of the equipment and any issues related to the store not being up to minimum standards. Responsibility for any repairs is then assigned.

One of these minimum standards involves the condition of mirrors in the bathrooms. In some locations, and this was one of them, there was a problem with vandals making deep scratches on the bathroom walls and mirrors. As we exited the bathroom, the company rep reminded me that it was our responsibility to put new mirrors in the bathrooms that met company standards. I expected this, and I had already ordered them.

But by this time, I had experience with McDonald's and with some of their managers. Consequently, I made the point that if McDonald's still owned the store at 11:59 p.m. that night, it was apparently okay for there to be damaged mirrors in the bathroom. But if I became an official franchisee at midnight and the new mirrors had not been put in place, I could be criticized for not complying with company standards. To some extent I was joking, but this was also something that could really happen.

We took over our second restaurant during the winter, and we immediately repaired the broken heating and air conditioning units. When we opened the restaurant on our first morning and turned on the heat, the regular customers who came in every morning for their coffee began to applaud. They said they couldn't remember when the heat had been working in the restaurant. We asked the regional management for an allowance to dress up the lobby, which was very dated.

The request was refused, but we were able to get fifteen thousand dollars from corporate to paint and replace some tabletops. When this restaurant was built, it included a basement. Two weeks after we took over, the main drain line, which ran along the ceiling, broke from the wall leading out to the street. When I called the regional manager to let him know that I would be sending him the bill, he asked, "How long will this go on?" To which I responded, "As long as we find issues of poor maintenance."

As cities grow and new shopping centers are built, an older location can be displaced from the mainstream. This became an issue with our second restaurant. A new shopping center was planned a mile and a half down the road. Fortunately, the developer was a friend and former city councilman. Before even one shovel of earth had been turned on the site, William shared with us the plans for the shopping center. He had a space specifically identified it for a fast-food brand and he wanted us to have it.

I called the McDonald's real estate reps for our area and described the opportunity. Since the location was in an underdeveloped and underserved part of the city, they were not at all familiar with it. After they drove through the neighborhood, the real estate reps felt it was not the right location for a McDonald's. But my opinion was the opposite.

I contacted Don Thompson, the newly appointed regional vice president, who was African American. After driving past the location and through the neighborhood with me, he agreed with me about the site. At a meeting in his office, Don signed the deal with William. We were going to relocate our second restaurant to the new shopping center.

One year after opening that store, our sales compared to the previous location increased by just under one million dollars. The McDonald's real estate department received an award for the successful relocation of a restaurant and the sales increase. But they felt so guilty that it had not been their decision that they included me in the recognition. Meanwhile, the old site was sold to the city for seven hundred fifty thousand dollars, none of which went into the new restaurant.

Sometimes a McDonald's employee on the corporate side of the business would switch to becoming a franchisee. This could only happen after being with the company for a significant number of years, and even then, the opportunity might not be the greatest. This would depend on your position, and ethnicity might also be a factor. Ray Aston was our field service manager and was African American. When he became a franchisee, he was sold was the lowest-volume restaurant in the market. Then, a few years later, he was awarded a new store being built in Murrieta, California. We were able to purchase his restaurant. We now had the lowest-volume restaurant in the city, which was also in the city's highest crime area.

Yet as time passed, our restaurants in African American communities became the most loyal and productive locations. That didn't happen by itself. Physically, these were older restaurants that showed some wear and tear. Also, training young employees in their first jobs is always a challenge in any neighborhood.

I had strong relationships with the San Diego city council and the mayor. I served on the advisory boards of three administrations. In 2000, the San Diego airport—Lindbergh Field—was beginning an expansion and a remodeling. The San Diego port commission had oversight of the airport. The chairman of the port commission, who was a friend and was African American, reached out to me and asked me to assist in writing the request for proposal.

At that time, the Federal Aviation Administration had developed a Disadvantaged Business Enterprise program to increase the minority business ownership in federally governed operations and contracts. The requirement had been in place for years, but companies were circumventing the requirement by using minorities as managers, which was not the intent.

For food concessions in the remodeled airport, any company that wanted a master contract would have to identify their minority partners in advance. For Tina and me, this meant that our good reputation in the African American community and in the whole city were valued assets. It also meant that McDonald's—which had always made the decision on who received a new site—would not be the decision maker here. If McDonald's wanted to get into the airport, it would be with us or there wouldn't be a McDonald's in the airport.

There was opportunity for three restaurants in the airport, one in each terminal. We were proposed for all three. We opened the first two restaurants six days apart and the third a year later.

Then an opportunity appeared to open a McDonald's on the Viejas Indian reservation and casino, thirty miles east of downtown San Diego. This too was an opportunity for which we were sought out. The chairman of the Viejas tribe was very involved with the NAACP in San Diego. He felt a kinship with African Americans, having gone through his own struggles of displacement, discrimination, and disrespect.

The tribal council wanted us to take over a location in which they were running their own hamburger restaurant. A McDonald's company representative visited the location and agreed, because the possibilities seemed attractive. McDonald's worked out the contracts, which were very complex. The Indian reservation was on sovereign land and could put McDonald's off the reservation at any time. We opened the first McDonald's on an Indian reservation west of the Mississippi.

By now, we had overcome the challenges of having the older stores. We had relocated one store and remodeled another. The high interest rates of the nineties had passed, and we felt we were on the upswing.

But an article in *Business Week* in 2003 described the corporation as "Hamburger Hell." The article outlined the story of an operator in Miami who, much like us, thought he had won the lottery when in 1973 he became a junior partner with McDonald's. Fast forward thirty years and he was the operator of four restaurants, but he said he was barely scrapping by. His sales hadn't budged since 1999 and the dollar menu featuring the Big N' Tasty burger had a negative impact on his bottom line.

In 1992, the NBMOA was formed, and by 1998 an agreement was being negotiated with the goal of raising the number of stores operated by African Americans to reflect the population of the communities they serve. It also took into account a disparity in profitability, which was lower on average compared to white franchisees. This was a very positive development, but at the same time, McDonald's was devoting too much energy to distractions that went nowhere.

In addition to experimenting with menu items, the company for some reason gave up its hugely successful slogan -- "You deserve a break today."—and during the 1990s it tried approximately forty new slogans. By 2000, when technology had become part of everyday life in business, McDonald's was slow to adapt. But a deal was made with First Data Corporation to take over cashless technology in the restaurants. I personally never understood why a company would be given a contract to tap into the finances of forty million customers per day and collect fees on millions of dollars, while the franchisees were expected to provide and pay for all the equipment this required. Along the way, Jack Greenberg, who had been CEO of McDonald's from 1999 through 2002, left McDonald's and became a director of First Data, and in 2006, became chairman of the board of Western Union, which was owned by First Data.

When we were operating six restaurants, there were several new opportunities for which we requested consideration, and we were denied. Fortunately, we were able to create other opportunities for ourselves through our relationships in the community.

Even so, we were behind in the number of stores and profitability in the restaurants we operated compared to most of the operators in the market. By 2003, all franchisees were feeling the pinch of shrinking margins that had dropped from a high of 15 percent to a paltry 4 percent. Top-down management made franchisees feel alienated from the corporation. This feeling was intensified by mandated reinvestment in projects such as the "Made for You" kitchen systems. We operated as efficiently as possible given the tight margins created by deep discounting.

CHAPTER 15

GIVING BACK

The one who blesses is abundantly blessed;
those who help others are helped.

—PROVERBS 11:25

Our oldest son, Jeremy, who was ten when we opened our first McDonald's, came into the office one day and told us that the ice machine was broken. I told him it was probably just recycling. It couldn't be broken because it was brand new. Jeremy left the office but came back a few minutes later insisting that the ice machine was broken. Tina told me to just go look. When I lifted the cover of the machine, I was hit in the face by sauna-like heat. The ice machine was broken all right. I apologized to Jeremy and never ignored him again.

Jeremy loved to work in the restaurant, especially taking orders in the drive-thru. He learned very quickly. He was standing by the employee taking orders and wearing a headset when we got a call from the child labor department. Someone had noticed Jeremy and called to report us. The child labor department was fine once we explained who Jeremy was.

We had been blessed with twins, Jonathan and Jennifer, in 1988. As an only child myself, I never wanted Jeremy to be without a brother or sister. As I stood by looking at the monitor on the day of Tina's ultrasound, the doctor said, "Do you see this heartbeat? And do you see *this* heartbeat?" It didn't register at first, and then I realized what he had just said. Tina and I both reacted at the same moment. We were shocked, but twins ran in Tina's family. Her grandmother was a twin herself, and then she became the mother of twins. I joked with the doctor that I had to go back to the restaurant and raise the prices.

By 1994, I was serving on several boards, including our local chapter of the Ronald McDonald House Charities. Across the country, the Ronald McDonald House Charities were governed and funded by local franchisees. The charity was involved in a wide variety of projects, large and small, and so were Tina and I. The owners were the founding partners in building the Child Abuse Prevention Center to fund grants to local schools. The owners also had an annual commitment to the local Ronald McDonald House. We raised funds in various ways, such as donating a portion of sales from items in the restaurants.

Every year at our owners' Christmas party, each owner would bring an item to be auctioned off and the proceeds donated to the charity. After a couple of years Tina came up with an idea for expanding the dinner and the auction. We had been limiting the amount of money we could raise by limiting the number of people who could buy items or put them up for bids. So, we changed this by including vendors and partners on our guest list.

Tina began a campaign of soliciting donations for the auction. She went to jewelers and department stores, while I went to some of my contacts for sports memorabilia, which was very popular with men. We had a good friend, Sid Brooks, who was the equipment manager for the San Diego Chargers. He was the first African American equipment manager in the NFL. I canvassed the restaurant owners and took orders for sports items that they wanted to see in the auction. Then Sid would get the items and donate them.

When San Diego hosted the Super Bowl, Sid oversaw the locker rooms and the ball boys for the game. As a result, we were able to auction off the opportunity to be a ball boy for the big game. This brought in a great deal of money, along with the auction of furs, jewelry, and over one hundred fifty other items. The auction became an annual event and our biggest fund-raiser. Tina and I would spend all year collecting items for the auction.

Our passion for raising money for any cause became a full-time job. For years, we had attended the McDonald's Gospel Fest in Los Angeles, which was put on by the Los Angeles store owners. We decided to do our own event in San Diego and selected Spreckels Theatre in downtown as the location. The theater held eleven hundred people and it was sold out in just a few days.

The second year we had to move to Symphony Hall, which had twenty-two hundred seats. This also sold out in several days. Except for the symphony performances, it was the first nonsecular event to be held there. We had choirs from Los Angeles, and even a prison choir. The event was organized to raise scholarship money for graduating high school students. San Diego Mayor Susan Golding attended and presented a special proclamation to McDonald's.

By this time, our work in San Diego had become well-known. Tina received a call one year after a devastating storm in Tijuana, Mexico. Makeshift houses had been washed away and families were homeless. Parents had taken their children to orphanages where they could have shelter.

When Mayor Golding asked Tina if McDonald's could do anything to help our sister city, Tina went into overdrive. She went to local businesses like Target, Payless Shoes, Golden State Foods, and Bama Foods (both McDonald's suppliers) and got food, clothing, and supplies for the families in need. She worked with the binational organization in Mexico to ensure that all the donations would go to those in need.

Golden State foods, our food supplier, was given special permission from the Mexican government to take an eighteen-wheeler across the border to deliver thirty thousand dollars' worth of goods. Along with some McDonald's employees, Tina and I went to Mexico and were escorted to a basketball arena where the goods would be distributed. As we were handing out the cots, food, blankets, and clothing, the children who had been left homeless arrived from the orphanage. We paused as the children took their seats in the stands.

Tina had received the names of each child, and we began to call them one by one to get their tennis shoes and socks donated by Payless Shoes. When the first little girl came up and sat on the floor to take off her old shoes, it was revealed that she had only the top parts of her socks. She wore the top parts of the socks so that no one would know that she didn't have a whole sock. As she put on her new socks and shoes, there wasn't a dry eye in the house.

Much had happened while we were working to grow our business. Tina began a scholarship program to help African American graduating high school students. She and her close girlfriend Debra Stevens, who passed away years ago, came up with the name AVAIL, for African American Visionary and Inspirational Leaders. Having received their 501(c) nonprofit status, the next step was coming up with money.

The President of McDonald's at that time was Ed Rensi, who had been part of Ray Kroc's original team. Ed had a great heart, and he believed in owners being part of a community and giving back to it. This was often called "polishing up the arches for McDonald's." At a national convention, Tina met with Ed about the scholarship program. Ed loved the idea and gave her ten thousand dollars to get started.

After the first couple of years, Tina wanted to give out more money. When she approached Ed again, he saw her coming, took his wallet out of his pocket, dropped it on the floor, and put his foot on it. By the time Tina got to him he was laughing. He said, "I don't have my wallet." Then he told Tina that if she needed money, all she had to do was call his secretary. He had put Tina in his budget.

The scholarship program soon got moved to the national Ronald McDonald House Charities Board in Chicago. After showing the success and impact that these scholarships were having, Tina envisioned a national program. If a local market raised twenty-five thousand dollars for scholarships, she proposed that the national charity match that amount to bring the scholarships to fifty thousand dollars per year.

This plan was adopted, and in the first year we were able to give fifty thousand dollars in scholarships. We started an awards breakfast to bring students, parents, teachers, and the superintendent of schools together to present the awards and recognize the students. We received a lot of press coverage for the program, but we also had some "haters." The company got several calls asking why there wasn't a program for White students.

Tina recognized that some people didn't see the urgent need to help these African Americans. So, she took up the challenge. She went to one of our market's White owners and asked him to chair a program for White students. She also went to Hispanic owners and asked them to start Hispanic scholarships. From that day to this, the AVAIL program has awarded more than nine hundred thousand dollars in scholarships.

When Jeremy was seventeen and in high school, and the twins were seven, we were very involved with our children's schools.

We still felt, however, that while our own kids had whatever they needed, we wanted to give a hand to those who were less fortunate. The Bible says, "to whom much is given, much is expected." We also felt that we needed our kids to understand how fortunate they were and to be involved with us in giving.

Each year at Thanksgiving we partnered with the mayor in a turkey giveaway at our restaurant. We ordered enough turkeys for our employees and for fifty families whom we identified as being in need. We also purchased gift cards from the supermarket so that the families could get all the holiday trimmings.

We also donated toys to the St. Vincent DePaul Center for a party at Christmas. I remember the first year that I brought Jeremy. He was around ten at the time. We brought Ronald McDonald along with us, which was a treat for the kids. The gifts were under the tree and when Ronald called out the names of the kids and they came up and picked out a gift. Jeremy assisted Ronald in handing out whatever was picked.

The first little boy who was called came up to the tree and picked out a bomber jacket, which were popular at the time. He grabbed the coat and hugged it with pure joy. Then I noticed a look of surprise on Jeremy's face. On our way home, I asked Jeremy how he felt about the day. When he said he enjoyed it, I inquired about his confused look with the first little boy. He said, "Well, I just didn't understand why he was so excited about a jacket." When I told him that that was probably the first new jacket that boy had ever had, Jeremy softly said, "Oh."

We also partnered with the fire and police departments for a Christmas giveaway to various nonprofits that would distribute the gifts to families. The kids loved this because we would go into the community on the hook-and-ladder fire truck with police escorts. It was fun for the kids, and it also created a foundation of giving and appreciation. This would serve them to this day, to be generous and share their blessings. My friend Tommy Dortch, who was chair of the 100 Black Men of America organization, used to have a saying that he used many times: "They will be what they see." Simple, profound, and true.

CHAPTER 16

TESTED

*I am convinced that life is 10% what happens to me
and 90% how I react to it.*

—CHARLES SWINDOLL

O ver the next few years we were immersed in the routines of our daily lives. But in 2000 we were tested, and I found myself thrown back into one of the most frightening times in my life. But whatever I felt, it was much worse for Tina. She found a lump in her breast. The cancer diagnosis instantly took me back to my mother's diagnosis. The memories of that diagnosis—of waiting for the results of the tests—came back as strongly as the impact the flowers had on me when my father died.

In the Black community of Los Angeles at that time, Dr. Weekes was the man to see. I don't believe that there was a black female who didn't go to Dr. Weekes. When my mother went in to have the lump removed, she had also given Dr. Weekes permission to do a radical mastectomy if the biopsy came back positive. She didn't want to have to go back in for another surgery. My aunt, who had a mastectomy surgery years before, advised that that was the best thing to do.

On the day of my mother's surgery, I went to the hospital to wait during the operation. My mother's sister was to meet me, but she was late and missed Dr. Weekes when he told me that he had to do the mastectomy.

I was rocked by that news. I went completely numb. It was as if I couldn't hear what he was saying. As I came out of the trance, I stood alone trying to figure out what to do. My mother was divorced at that time, but we had kept a good relationship with Les, my stepfather. I went to the pay phone and called him. It was all I could do to repeat what Dr. Weekes had told me.

I broke down on the phone as Les tried to tell me that everything would be okay. His consoling me did help somewhat. By the time my mother was brought to her room, the anesthetic had worn off. She was heavily bandaged, but she couldn't tell what procedure had been done. I managed to say that they had done a mastectomy. As her eyes welled up with tears, I was silent for a moment, not knowing what to say.

Then her sister arrived. As I told her what the doctor had said, she hugged my mother and I took the opportunity to step out of the room and collect myself. I knew that my breaking down was not going to help.

My mother was, of course, afraid of further surgery, and the myth that surgery could spread the disease. In the end, she chose to have radiation treatments rather than chemotherapy.

She was concerned about the effects of the treatment, and also about losing her hair. As it turned out, her cancer was a relatively non-aggressive cancer and she would not have a recurrence for thirteen years. With the protocols and advances available today she most likely would have survived without ever having a reoccurrence.

Tina's diagnosis took me back to that terrible time. In some ways it was even more difficult than how I felt as a child when my father died. That had been frightening and mysterious, but now I knew the facts—the hard facts—of what was really happening.

We bought a home in La Costa just north of San Diego. It was in a great neighborhood, though predominantly White with only a few African Americans in the area. Our neighbors were wonderful, and Jeremy made lots of friends.

One evening he came into my office at home and seemed very timid, which was unusual for Jeremy. I asked what was wrong and he said, "I just wanted you to know what happened at Warehouse Records today."

He continued on to say that he and his friend Alvin had ridden their bikes to the store to buy a CD. After he bought his CD and left the store, he was going to call home to let us know he was on his way back when the assistant manager came outside and told the two boys to come back into the store. Inside, the manager said that someone had seen them steal the CDs.

Both boys had passed through the metal detector when they left the store and again when reentered, and they had receipts for the CDs. But they were made to open their bags and take everything out. When nothing suspicious was found, the manager made them pull up their pants and shirts. This happened in the middle of the store in view of all the other customers. Finally, the boys were allowed to leave.

I went ballistic. I jumped in the car with Jeremy and went back to the store. The manager had left so I spoke to the assistant manager who had done the search. First, I loudly demanded that the manager get called back to the store. Then, I asked the assistant manager what right he had to strip search my son? When he asked if we could go into his office, I said, "No way, we're going to talk here right where you stripped searched my son."

By this time the manager of the store had arrived. He asked for an explanation of what had happened, and then I agreed to go into his office with the assistant manager. As soon as the office door was closed, I was nose to nose with the young man who had embarrassed my son. It was more than just anger. I wanted him to feel what Jeremy felt when he and his friend were searched.

Both the manager and the assistant manager were apologetic, but I asserted that it was illegal to bring the boys back into the store on the assumption that they had stolen something. I gave them my business card and left.

No sooner was I home than I got a call from the district manager. He had gotten the story and he too wanted to apologize. I simply told him that this kind of profiling was unacceptable, and they would hear from us. We settled the case shortly thereafter.

We were living in an upscale community of well-educated people. But stereotypical attitudes and behaviors still followed us. At Jeremy's school, we contributed food for fundraisers and worked at various events. Still, Jeremy came to me with concerns about being made to sit in an assigned seat on the bus to school. He said that a group of boys were goofing off in the back of the bus so the driver made several of them sit up front so she could keep an eye on them. This included Jeremy and his friend Alvin, who was also Black.

I told him that they shouldn't be fooling around on the bus. He said that he wasn't fooling around, but he got pulled into what the other kids were doing. At any rate, he said all the other boys had been allowed to sit anywhere they wanted but he and Alvin were required to sit in the front. This had been going on for weeks.

All this had a powerful effect on me. Maybe it was because seating on a bus has such a history for African Americans in general, and I was also very aware of Tina's experiences with busses in Louisiana.

The next morning, I told Jeremy that he should refuse to sit in the assigned seat on the bus. Then I parked down the street. When the bus arrived, I saw him get on the bus and then get right back off. He had tried to choose his own seat, and the driver had told him he couldn't ride. When the bus left him standing on the street, I picked him up and drove straight to the school. We got there before the school bus arrived. I asked the vice principal to come out of his office and together we waited for the bus.

While we were waiting, I informed the vice president what had been happening. When the bus arrived, I noticed that a security guard had been assigned to ride the bus. There was obviously already some awareness of a problem.

By midday, television and radio news had gotten hold of the story from the local Urban League. As a consequence, the entire school district was put through a series of programs that included sensitivity training. This was implemented by Stedman Graham, a longtime friend.

This was not the end. When Jeremy got his driver's license, he was stopped twelve times in his first year on the road. It was a case of driving while being young and Black. Since we lived in La Costa, his car was naturally registered with a La Costa address. Jeremy would often drive to southeast San Diego to play basketball. This was in the same predominately African American neighborhood as our restaurant. When the police saw him driving in that area, they would run his license plates and when the registration came back with a La Costa address they would pull him over. They'd ask for the registration, and on one occasion the officer sarcastically remarked, "It must be nice to have a car like this at sixteen," and let him go.

After Jeremy was repeatedly stopped, we made an appointment with the police chief, whom we knew well. We shared our concerns about the profiling of young Black men, and the consequences of suspended driver's licenses and canceled insurance. This could mean not being able to get to school or to work.

A policy was put in place requiring a contact card to be filled out for every police stop. When the cards were reviewed, it was clear that young African Americans were stopped far more than other groups. Jeremy and I were asked to visit the police commands in the neighborhoods to speak with the officers. I was struck by the fact that several of the officers had stopped Jeremy so often they knew him by sight and by name.

Through all of this, I felt an obligation to change perceptions, change minds, change attitudes, with the most important goal of changing actions. Because of the respect that Tina and I had gained in the community, we were to make ourselves heard on behalf of those who otherwise might be ignored.

After Jeremy graduated from high school, he attended San Diego State University. Since he played on the basketball team, he was given housing in a condo in an area of the campus where athletes lived. It had a living room, two bedrooms, and a balcony. When we visited him in his assigned unit and asked what he thought of it, he said, "Well, it's okay."

Because I knew that Jeremy had been spoiled in many ways, I took him to look at some of the nonathlete dorms at SDSU. I showed him the rooms and the shower down the hall that everyone on the whole floor shared. The rooms had no balconies. Jeremy got my point but still didn't really apply himself during his first year. He played basketball and got the perks that went along with that.

During Jeremy's second semester I got a call from his coach. The school tried to give athletes every advantage by providing tutors and study halls, but Jeremy wasn't showing up. That night I went to the school and drove Jeremy's car home.

He called me the next morning and said his car had been stolen. When I told him that I had taken it, he was shocked, to say the least.

He asked, "How am I going to get around?"

I said, "Get a bicycle."

"What about when it rains?"

"Get an umbrella."

Tina and I wanted the best for our kids, but we realized that we had sheltered them too much. They needed more connection to their heritage. Life had been very different for past generations of their family. For his second year, we moved Jeremy to Fisk University, a smaller, predominately Black school in Nashville, Tennessee.

When he called home, Jeremy said he was having a great time and enjoying being around so many students who looked like him. He felt empowered and connected to his blackness. The only thing he found frustrating was that he couldn't get pizza delivered to the campus after dark.

When Jeremy started playing basketball at a relatively high level, I tried to impress upon him the importance of not planning on being a professional athlete. I said the same thing to Jeremy's friends who were aspiring to the NBA. Fortunately, my message to Jeremy was reinforced when he heard the same thing from some friends who played for the Los Angeles Lakers.

When Jeremy returned from Fisk, he entered what's called McDonald's Second Generation program. Everyone who wants to become a franchisee, including children of current owners, must go through the same training as their parents. There is no guarantee that legacy applicants will be approved. Everyone needs to meet the same standards.

Around this same time, Tina and I found ourselves at our own crossroads. We needed to decide where we wanted to retire. Opportunities for us in San Diego did not look promising. Fast food was a mature market. There would not be many new stores opening, and we had already been passed up before.

Our friend Don Thompson was now president of McDonald's. He understood our frustrations in San Diego, and he was not surprised when I told him we wanted to relocate. I told Don that if any opportunity came up in Las Vegas, we would be interested.

We now had a second home in Las Vegas, which is very business friendly with no state tax. Before long, we received a call about a Las Vegas opportunity. At that time, we had three restaurants and looked to get another three in Vegas.

In San Diego, we met with the director of operations for company stores in the Las Vegas area. Here again we encountered corporate America's constant issue with how we lived as African Americans. The director of operations introduced himself and immediately said, "I understand that your house is in Turnberry."

Yes, our house was in Turnberry, one of the most exclusive areas of Vegas. But where we lived had nothing to do with what this meeting was about. This man was supposed to describe the restaurants that McDonald's was going to sell us. But for him, the issue was Turnberry. It was the same old story: How did you get here, and how could you be living where White people live?

We managed to get past that. He told us about the stores that were being sold, and we made plans to fly to Vegas and see the properties. When we arrived there and drove to the restaurants, we were upset and disappointed. The stores were old and in rough areas of the city. They were also near a military base that might be closing, which would take away the main customer source for the restaurants.

Back in San Diego, I spoke to the regional manager about our displeasure with what was offered. He said he would look into it, as he was not aware of the specific restaurants.

I agreed and a few weeks later we were back in Vegas with a very different perspective. Eleven restaurants were now made available to us, and we bought six of them. At this time, the twins were both in college. Jennifer was a freshman at the University of Nevada, Las Vegas and Jonathan was at the College of Art and Design in Laguna, California. Our director of operations was in San Diego and our office manager would be coming with us to Vegas, and we helped them relocate.

CHAPTER 17

WHAT STAYS IN VEGAS

*Too many of us are not living our dreams
because we are living our fears.*

—LES BROWN

One thing we never expected coming to the Vegas market was the obvious resentment that some in the corporation had for us. In one of the stores we had purchased, the field service team had for all practical purposes trashed the store. The managers who now worked for us opened the store to find that all the training and operational manuals had been removed from the office. The telephones had been taken out, all the office supplies had been taken, and the clock on the wall had been removed. Some of the equipment for which we had signed off had been swapped for older equipment from other corporate stores. Uniforms and spare parts that had been ordered had also been thrown out.

When we reviewed the security tapes, we clearly saw the field service people in action, basically wrecking the store. My first thought was, Why? Why would they do this? The answer would appear over the coming years, when we experienced much of the same double standard that we had faced in San Diego.

We realized that this spirit of discrimination had become woven into the very fabric of the corporation, until it was almost second nature to the personnel. They gave no more thought to it than other things they did every day.

We, as minorities, were simply not deserving of the opportunities or respect that everyone else received. When we brought these slights to people's attention, we were labeled as arrogant, militant, and just plan angry Black people.

When I notified the director of field services and explained what had happened to our store, he was clearly shocked and embarrassed. By the next day he made sure that we got back all the training and operational materials that we required to operate the restaurant. He offered to replace the office supplies and clocks, but I had already replaced most of the items that were needed immediately.

In the Las Vegas of old, even Black entertainers who starred in casino shows couldn't stay in the hotels where they were working. Similarly, McDonald's had little experience with African American operators in Las Vegas, and those operators were disrespected as if by reflex. When we arrived in Vegas, there were only two other African American operators in the metro area.

I would come to realize that another source of resentment toward us was our close friendship with Don Thompson, who would become the president of McDonald's, and later the CEO. Don had helped us get to Las Vegas, but we certainly had not gotten any special, high-volume restaurants. On the contrary, except for one, the stores we were sold were well below the national average volume.

Large American corporations, including McDonald's, always have a good-old-boy network, but this had never worked in our favor. We always worked hard to earn everything we had. In fact, we had purposely not tried to use our friendship with Don in any way. We were determined to avoid any appearance of special favors. If anything, we had hurt ourselves by not taking advantage of the friendship.

As we embarked in Las Vegas on a new chapter in our lives, we thought that we would have a break from the pressure of being the largest African American McDonald's operator in San Diego. For the past twenty-one years, that community had counted on us for jobs and for support of many local organizations in the community.

But our break from carrying responsibility for the community was a short-lived idea in Las Vegas. With our daughter attending UNLV, we became very involved with the university and in our church. Tina would be selected to serve on the trustee and foundation boards for UNLV. Through the church, we continued the annual scholarship program that Tina had started in San Diego, and after Jennifer's graduation we established a scholarship endowment at UNLV in our daughter's name.

After a year in Las Vegas, we were offered two more restaurants, and a year later there were two more. This brought us to a total of nine. We had never asked Don Thompson for any special treatment or consideration, but through the years we were always aware of how this friendship had been perceived.

Tina and I had attended the Trumpet Awards in Atlanta for several years. The founder of the awards, Xenoma Clayton, was an executive for Ted Turner with offices at the CNN Center. She had a long friendship with Ted and they would usually start each morning by having coffee together.

Xernona had also been a personal assistant to Dr. King in the 1960s and was a close friend of his family. She had driven Dr. King to the airport for his trip to Memphis, where he would be assassinated. She had helped Mrs. King arrange the funeral and assisted Mrs. King when calls came in from all over the world. Subsequently, she went to work with Ted Turner, representing the company in Atlanta and across the country.

Even before Oprah, Xernona was the first African American women to host her own television talk show. With Ted Turner's support and financial backing, Xernona created the Trumpet Awards as an annual televised event recognizing the achievements of African Americans, as well as the contributions of those who have furthered the progress of the African American cause.

In 2004, Xernona Clayton was given the opportunity to own the rights to the Trumpet Awards, and she was given an endowment for a nonprofit foundation to carry on the program. I was blessed by Ms. Clayton to be asked to be the chairman of the foundation.

This opportunity would prove to be a most impactful experience for my whole family. In school or elsewhere, my generation had never been educated about the African American experience. When my children entered school,

Black history was finally starting to be taught.

My family and I were honored to meet many of the leaders who paved the way for change in the United States. We met Rosa Parks, C.T. Vivian, Ambassador Andrew Young, John Lewis, members of the Congressional Black Caucus, and Mrs. King and the King family. To have a conversation with someone like Ambassador Young was more than a history lesson. It was like earning a PhD in appreciation for those whose sacrifices—sometimes with their lives—have enabled us to come as far as we have. They were educators, scientists, authors, physicians, and other outstanding citizens in every walk of life whose contributions often went unrecognized.

When Don Thompson was in line to be the CEO of McDonald's, a very positive step was Don's receiving the Trumpet Award as executive of the year. While he was liked and respected by the franchisees,

Tina, Rosa Parks, and Harold

it was also important that he have recognition outside the company. The Trumpet Award was a great fulfillment of that need.

When the CEO of McDonald's announced his upcoming retirement, everyone was eager to know who would succeed him. Don had been the right hand of the CEO. He was respected by the shareholders and Wall Street. He seemed to be the front runner.

We were in a symposium with McDonald's National Black Operators Association when one of the owners brought up the topic of the next CEO. He felt that the executive board of the organization should ask for a meeting with the CEO and demand that Don get the job. This immediately struck me as a bad idea. I stepped out of the meeting and called Don Thompson to express my concern, and Don agreed with me.

I returned to the meeting and stood at the back of the room while the topic was debated. When I caught the eye of the chairwoman, I shook my head no and then asked that this be tabled for future discussion by the executive board. This was agreed upon.

That night I called the Black Operators chairwoman, and I also called the past chairman. I said that I had spoken with Don and he agreed that approaching the CEO was not a good idea. I was able to be very frank on both those calls.

I said, "You don't go in to meet with the CEO and demand he make the decision you want. He will most likely do just the opposite."

I suggested to the chairwoman that she call the CEO to wish him well in his retirement, and to thank him for his support of our organization. She could state our obvious hope that Don would become the next CEO, but we would fully support whoever was selected. As it turned out, Don Thompson was appointed as the next CEO. Shortly after the announcement, the chairwoman of the Black Operators Association received a call from the retiring CEO. He indicated that he appreciated her earlier call and the support she offered.

I have learned over the years that in corporate life, in the life of an entrepreneur, and in life as a Black man that tact and finesse can help a person make the decision you want, by letting them think it was their decision all along.

CHAPTER 18

REVELATION AND UNDERSTANDING

There is nothing worse than a sharp image
of a fuzzy concept.

—ANSEL ADAMS

By 2011, Jeremy had finished McDonald's Second Generation program. He had purchased a restaurant from us and become a franchisee. By selling him one of our restaurants, we could set and discount the price. If he bought from another owner or from the corporation, the price wouldn't be discounted. Jennifer had graduated from UNLV. She and Jonathan were both living in Las Vegas and had come into the business.

Jonathan and Jennifer had been born into McDonald's, so this was all they knew. Jonathan majored in art and has sold some of his work, but he wanted to continue the lifestyle he had grown up with. He didn't want to be a starving artist. He felt he could have the best of both worlds by staying with McDonald's and by painting too.

Several years earlier, unknown to me, Jonathan had told his brother, his sister, and his mother that he was gay. Now he finally sat down and shared this with me.

My first concern, as well as Tina's, was for Jonathan's safety in an intolerant world. Along with that, what hurt me to the core was not the revelation but the fact that for years he had not wanted us to know because he thought we would disown him. We had known friends who had done just that when they found out about their own kids.

It was almost unbearably painful to realize that my son imagined that my love was not unconditional. It hurt me that he had even had even a second of fear that I would turn my back on him. I reassured him of my love for him and that nothing would ever change that. I could almost see the relief come over him, as if he had been holding his breath for years and finally could exhale.

This experience changed me drastically. We all, in our youth, have made fun or looked down on someone who was different from us. I had never really had any prejudice against anyone, and I had many gay friends and colleagues in work. Still, my son had feared rejection.

After this realization, I found myself looking at everyone with a softer heart. I became more empathetic, aware, and caring than ever before. Yet I thought I had always been that way.

I went back to the Bible to really assess myself. I found that if you believe the first three words in the bible—"In the beginning"—you must believe everything that comes after that comes from God, and the Bible also says that God makes no mistakes.

Because I believed this, I knew that God had made Jonathan just as He had made me and everyone else. I could never forsake Jonathan any more than God would.

This whole experience strengthened my ability to help my aunt, who was then in treatment for pancreatic cancer. She was my father's youngest brother's wife and was just a few years older than me. She had known me since I was ten. Jennifer and I went to see her a few weeks before she passed. While we were there, she asked that we talk privately. She was very religious and was troubled with trying to come to terms with her daughter being gay. We had both grown up in a church and a society that looked at this as an abomination. It was a topic people didn't even want to talk about.

She didn't want to leave without a reconciliation of her feelings for her daughter. She was trying to find a way toward acceptance, while still being true to her faith. We can all become conflicted with the interpretations of the scriptures, from church to church and faith to faith.

I shared with her my experience with Jonathan. I reminded her that we had been brought up in a God-loving and God-fearing family. I told her about my thoughts on the first three words in the Bible and how I had come to terms with myself as much as with Jonathan. Our eyes welled up. We were so very close, and as we looked at each other, I felt the years of our lives flash before me.

She thanked me for what I had shared with her and said she felt at peace with her daughter. She just wanted her to be happy and to live a good life, as I wanted for Jonathan. I felt that although there was nothing more I could do for her now, I had given her what she needed at the time and felt good about it.

Jennifer's situation was different from her brothers'. She had graduated with honors, majoring in hotel management. She too was used to a certain lifestyle, but she also didn't want to work for someone and take time to advance in a new company. She wanted to be her own boss.

Both Jonathan and Jennifer had made their own significant contacts while in college. While visiting Los Angeles, one of Jonathan's friends took him to meet a young man whom she knew. She had told her friend about our family. His name was Lemmie

Plummer. He and his brother had been in a development contract with BET, producing reality shows.

Lemmie met Jonathan and admitted that he didn't know that Black people even owned McDonald's. Lemmie and his brother came to Las Vegas to meet our family and we immediately connected with them. We were also impressed that these two young men—who were the same age as our children—had such impressive resumes.

After spending some time with us, Lemmie asked if we would like to produce a "sizzle reel" that could be used in a pitch for a reality show about our family. Naturally, our kids were all over this. Tina and I ultimately agreed, and I wrote a check to Lemmie for what he needed to create the reel.

Lemmie was shocked that I would show such trust in him. I told him that we were a family of faith and felt an immediate confidence in him and his brother. We would learn later that he was raised in a faith-based family and his father was a minister. Lemmie and his brother left that Saturday and returned on Monday to start the production.

We spent several days shooting. When we were shown the final sizzle, I felt the talent behind this project was unbelievable. The show was shopped to various networks, and one of the biggest companies in the reality category wanted to do our show.

But how was McDonald's going to react? We had been telling our story in many magazines and TV interviews every year, especially during Black History month. Our family story was also videotaped for the Black History Makers exhibit, which is permanently archived at the Library of Congress.

Tina and I had done interviews, served on televised panels, and had even done a commercial for McDonald's—so the concern was not our loyalty and credibility. Rather, the issue was how the McDonald's brand would be shown. Don Thompson was now the

CEO, but I got a call from the president of the company. She was very concerned with the show being "about McDonald's." I explained that this should be understood as a positive view of the opportunities that McDonald's had given to so many African American owners.

McDonald's vice president of marketing was more concerned about the portrayal of being a franchisee. He wanted to show the hard work of it. He didn't want the public to think that we were making too much money. This struck me as extremely hypocritical. The company's profits were available to the public, as were the salaries of the officers of the company. But God forbid anybody should think that franchisees were making money.

After much discussion, we moved forward with the network and agreed on a contract. Then one day I got a call from McDonald's legal department with some serious concerns. They shared with me that in a conversation with the network's attorney, he was asked what kinds of things would be shown in the program.

The network attorney said, "Well, we might want to show the franchisee running through the restaurant chasing a rat with a broom."

When I heard this, I immediately called the network and asked them if they had gone crazy. I said, "I would never have something like that happen in my restaurant, and certainly would not do a film that would hugely damage the McDonald's brand."

But a close look at the contract showed they would have the right to show anything that they might shoot without our approval. With that, we pulled out of the deal.

But the story wasn't over. Lemmie had told me of his desire to start his own company. He had become discouraged by working for networks where his ideas and projects were taken and controlled by his employers. He was not getting the credit he felt he deserved. One afternoon, we sat in my home with Johnathan Rogers, who had most recently been the CEO of TV-ONE and prior to that the president of the CBS TV stations group. We viewed some of the shows that Lemmie had produced. We also saw the obvious talent behind the shows, and we decided to give financial backing to a new production company. It would be called L. Plummer Media.

We immediately started working on shows to pitch. Our first was *Preachers of L.A.* Its first broadcast was the highest-rated premier on its network. From there came *Preachers of Detroit*; *Preachers of Atlanta*; *The Westbrooks*; *Living with Funny*; *Music Moguls*; and *Two Sides*, in partnership with Viola Davis's company.

In 2018 we would launch a new social media platform called ZEUS. It would be a disrupter in the social media space and the future of social media streaming.

With the success of these shows, the company was in demand. Instead of asking for meetings to pitch our projects, we were now taking calls from people who wanted to meet with us.

Meanwhile, the revisions and reinvestments at McDonald's would continue. Whenever there was a new initiative, there was also a cost. The cooking procedures were changed—cooking on a clamshell grill, for example, which allowed meat to be cooked on both sides. This was an initiative to speed up service. But we had to throw out perfectly good grills to replace them with the new one. And this did not guarantee any additional profit on the bottom line.

The company was adding new products to the menu, such as frappes and espresso coffee. This required new equipment and construction to accommodate the new equipment. The coffee initiative was a monster promotion, with the system giving away millions of free samples to draw in new customers.

It was always troubling when we, at the store level, were required to give away free samples but the suppliers didn't participate in the giveaway. We had to purchase the coffee, and then give it away free.

The real kicker was how, after stores had given away millions of cups of free coffee to draw in new customers, the company began packaging the coffee and selling it in supermarkets. Now people could buy the coffee and make it at home. It was especially disheartening to see McDonald's coffee on the shelves of a supermarket in the same shopping center as our restaurant. It would have been so simple to let the restaurants sell the coffee and at least share in the results of all the promotion.

The reimagining of restaurant exteriors was the most extensive and expensive program to date. The look of the buildings had been the same forever, but how did this affect revenues for the stores? While the company participated in the program, it was still an investment for the franchisees that, in many cases, did not generate big financial returns. People wouldn't necessarily come to the restaurant because it looked new. They should come for the food, which needed to be the driver.

We wanted our buildings to look great but making that happen added to our debt—and we were reinvesting in a building that we didn't own. This also increased the value of the buildings, which increased the property taxes we had to pay.

CHAPTER 19

JEREMY AND FRIEND

When someone shows you who they are,
believe them the first time.

—MAYA ANGELOU

While we were managing all these initiatives, Jeremy was not showing the kind of dedication to the business that Tina and I had always given. He was seeing a young lady he had met in Las Vegas. She and her sister were living in Los Angeles. When I met her, I was unfortunately (but totally) under impressed.

She was a rather well-known entertainer in Romania who was trying to start a career in the United States. When Tina met her, she was even more concerned than I was. But we had learned from Jeremy that the more we protested a relationship, the more determined he was to continue it.

For a short time, she and her sister moved to Las Vegas. Because Jeremy didn't have a nine-to-five job, he gave the impression that the restaurant just ran itself. It was not long before she and her sister moved back to Los Angeles, and for a while Jeremy commuted.

Some McDonald's owners have restaurants in several states, and some don't even live in the same state as their restaurants. We had wanted Jeremy to be physically working in his restaurant to prepare for running the entire organization with Jonathan and Jennifer.

In this respect, the company had always wanted more from us than other owners, and we had delivered it. Now McDonald's naturally expected that Jeremy would be in the restaurant every day, although that wasn't required of other owners. Meanwhile, our director of operations, who had moved to Las Vegas with us, became ill. She had been a heavy drinker as a teen and it had now caught up with her. She was on the waiting list for a liver transplant.

This accelerated Jennifer's responsibilities, as she stepped into the director of operation's role. Jonathan was managing his own restaurant. At the same time, as an organization we were also collectively overseeing Jeremy's location. This put a lot of responsibility on Jennifer and Jonathan. They naturally resented Jeremy not pulling his share of the load.

As Jeremy commuted back and forth to Los Angeles, we could see the strain it was having on everyone in the family. Then one day we were all at lunch and Jeremy announced that his girlfriend was pregnant. He insisted he loved her and was happy they were going to have a baby.

We had always felt that she had come to America to find a "sugar daddy." Her sister was here in an arranged marriage with an American, for the sole purpose of getting citizenship. It was apparent to Tina and me that she was after the same thing. If Jeremy was aware of this, he didn't admit it.

Tina and I agreed that we had to do everything we could to make this work out as well as possible. Jeremy and his girlfriend decided they wanted to get married and they announced their engagement. When we sat down with the two of them, we wanted to be positive.

This was going to be our first grandchild. We had mixed emotions, of course, but we were going to give them all the support we could.

We didn't want money spent on an engagement ring. After talking it over, Tina and I offered the ring that I had given Tina when we got engaged. We also made it clear that if for any reason the marriage didn't happen, the ring would be returned. Am I foolish, or stupid, or both?

As the birth of the baby approached, Jeremy spent more time in Los Angeles. She was having a C-section, so we were able to plan to be in Los Angeles for the birth. Noah was born November 6, 2011. Jeremy had told us that they would be moving back to Vegas, so we prepared a nursery in the condo where Jeremy lived.

Jeremy had cousins in Los Angeles who were in the music business. While he and her were there, he got his cousins to cut a demo for her. This was an effort to help launch her career in the United States. While the cousins were putting time into this, they moved back to Las Vegas.

It became clear to us that, when Jeremy married her, he was also getting a sister-in-law to support. We had told him we knew that she was too attached to her sister, but Jeremy disagreed. He insisted that her sister wanted to be on her own.

After Noah was born, she naturally wanted her mother to see the baby. It was very difficult in Romania to get an exit visa if there are other family members already in the United States. There is a concern that the traveler won't return. Again, to be supportive, we drafted a letter to the Romanian consulate ensuring that her mother would be staying with us and that she would return.

Whatever it was that tipped the scale, her mother was allowed to visit. We had everyone over for Christmas, as Christmas dinner was a family tradition. Tina even gave Jeremy's Fiance's mother a beautiful shawl as a gift.

Right after Christmas, it was announced that Jeremy's wife wanted to move back to Los Angeles. She was totally out of touch with reality. She believed that Jeremy didn't have to work.

We had only seen Noah a few times after Christmas before they returned to Los Angeles. Tina always reminds us that she never even got to change Noah's diaper. The baby never slept in the nursery that we had made for him. Over the next year, we would see Noah for only a day or two when they came to Vegas. We were glad that we were at least able to have Noah's first birthday celebration at our home.

Soon after his first birthday, Jeremy's fiancée announced that she had to go back to Romania to renew her visa. We again drafted a letter supporting her prompt return to the United States and the possibility of getting work here. She wanted Jeremy to accompany her, but we were firm that he had to stay and run his business.

By now, Jeremy was resigned to the fact that his wife was never going to separate from her sister, and that three people in a marriage was one too many. For her part, she decided that the ring that we had given them needed to be enhanced. It was a two-carat, pear-shaped diamond. We had stressed to them that they should not spend money on things that weren't necessary, and they definitely should not spend money they didn't have on a ring. Of course, that advice fell on deaf ears. She took the ring to a jeweler she knew and had it redesigned.

When Jeremy told us that he didn't feel that it was going to work out with her, I emphatically told him to get the ring from the jeweler before she left for Romania. But Jeremy let me know that that couldn't happen. They owed money on the ring and the jeweler wouldn't release it. Of course, when she departed, she had gotten the ring out without paying for it, assuring the jeweler that Jeremy would come by to pay for it later.

We have not seen nor heard from her in more than five years. She won't communicate or send pictures. Noah will be six this year. The pictures we have seen are those that our kids find on the Internet when she posts them. Since we don't have any diplomatic relations with Romania, we have no recourse. Jeremy would love to go to Romania, but with the corrupt system in that country, we would never allow him to go there and possibly be detained.

Jonathan reached out to a reporter in Romania and because his wife is a Romanian celebrity, he got a return call. After telling the reporter the story of what happened here, several articles appeared that blasted her. All those articles are on the Internet and our hope is that someday Noah will be able to look to them up, find his father and his family, and know that he was not abandoned. Hardly a day goes by when Noah is not in our thoughts, and we can only imagine the pain that Jeremy feels at not being part of his son's life. We know too that he deeply regrets our losing our first grandchild. But he keeps so much to himself. Jeremy has moved on and met a wonderful woman who loves him. They are there for each other and are building a wonderful life together. He will reunite with Noah someday and will tell him about his family and grandparents who loved him.

CHAPTER 20

LETTING GO

Forget what hurt you but never forget
what it taught you.

—SHANNON L. ALDER

In 2014, McDonald's built two restaurants that were close to the trade area of three of our Las Vegas stores. While we were not offered these locations, I felt that even if they had been offered to us, they would impact our existing stores and potentially hurt our sales and profitability. As I expected, when the two new stores opened, our stores' sales declined by 10 percent each.

Cannibalization of sales by other McDonald's restaurants has been a historical problem with the company. With the impact of the new stores, plus the sales decline that the entire system was experiencing at that time, we were quickly burning through our reserves. When we contacted the company about what was happening, the response was to evaluate the problem and take that information to an impact committee composed of both corporate officials and operators.

That group would make a determination about the financial effects of one store on another. Once the financial impact was assessed, the company would then express that as a dollar amount that would be reimbursed. The catch was that the operator would not get the money to directly reimburse the loss. The operator would be required to put together a plan on how he or she would spend the money on a marketing plan or on remodeling the restaurant to rebuild the lost sales. You wouldn't recoup lost cash flow to help pay your debt, or your payroll, or whatever else was needed to run your operation. You had to spend the money to regain the sales that you had built up over the years, or otherwise reinvest the money in the company's asset.

While this evaluation was taking place, we put together a plan to eliminate underperforming stores from our organization. Over the next eighteen months we had multiple meetings and conference calls with the company about this. At one of the first meetings in Las Vegas, we addressed what we saw as a focused effort to depict us in a negative light, by trying to prevent our recognition with the 365 Black Award. This was in addition to damaging our organization by building stores that took away our sales.

In the first meeting, we were presented with the option of McDonald's buying us out. We understood at that point that there was a basic intention to get us out of the system. On our side, we proposed an exchange of stores, with the company taking over and selling our impacted restaurants and then selling us a company store that was also in our trading area. Meanwhile, while all these meetings were going on, we were bleeding cash flow. And McDonald's itself was experiencing some of the most negative sales results in years, and the company's stock was on a downward trend.

Don Thompson, who was McDonald's CEO, had explicitly requested that this situation be promptly corrected. Because Don

McDonald's 365 Black Award, presented to Harold and Tina

could not get personally involved in the process, he assigned the president of the company for US operations to address it. At the national convention in 2012, we met with the president, who assured us he would take care of the situation. He hugged us and said, "Who loves you?" Right then, I should have known we were in trouble. He was fired a few weeks later. We next met with the COO, who brought up the buyout. We hadn't had much hope that the COO would be of any assistance, since the general manager had told him that we shouldn't receive the 365 Black Award. Yet she herself came to New Orleans to present the award to us.

During the next year, we had the COO, the US operations president, the chief financial officer, and the general manager of our region all involved in our situation. It should have been very simple, especially since McDonald's needed its executives to focus on the currently poor performance of the company systemwide.

Our problems persisted simply because the individuals who could have solved the problems had no desire to do so. The fact that we had challenged instances of poor decision making in the company, as well as our friendship with Don Thompson and his intervening on our behalf, was resented by the McDonald's establishment. They knew that Don, as CEO, could not get directly involved, so stalling with us was a convenient way to tweak Don.

If one of the previous CEOs had asked that our situation be fixed, it would have been done right away. To me, this was clearly resentment from many in top management for Don being the CEO. I believed they were eager to prolong any mess that might come up, with the expectation that Don would be blamed for it and would not be the CEO for long.

Several changes were already taking place. After the president for US operations was fired, the newly appointed US president was making his moves. The COO, who had earlier fired the president, was fired by a new president, upon which the position of COO was eliminated.

At the end of the day, our deal was taken to the US president by the National Black McDonald's Operators Association board of directors. An agreement was reached, and we sold our stores back to the company.

By standing on principal and being outspoken, we had become expendable to the system. Don would submit his resignation, which alerted us to the ascendency of those who resented our friendship with him. Those same people further resented Don's intervention in the past against the unfair treatment that we had experienced. This was all a matter of getting back at us, and of getting back at Don Thompson.

If it had not been for the NBMOA, we never would have been able to leave the system with what we did. Unfortunately, this was also a divisive experience among the NBMOA board members. Fortunately, most understood the situation we had been put in and we worked hard to clarify what the solution should be.

The NBMOA organization did not have the same respect from the company that it once had. The company took for granted the many contributions that the Black operators made. The sad part for us was how the opportunity for our children to come into the system had been diminished. We became entrepreneurs and built a legacy that the company was taking away.

Our story, which can be read online and in the many articles written about us, benefited and elevated the McDonald's brand both in the United States and internationally. The brand had fundamentally diverged from Ray Kroc's original vision. Family was no longer a priority, whether it was the family of McDonald's franchisees or the families who were McDonald's core customers. Instead, the brand had become all about Wall Street's investment firms and the large real estate trusts that hold so much of McDonald's stock.

We, the operators, had become not just sharecroppers—we had always been that—but slaves to the system and its leadership, which governed with a malignant heart. Profit became the rule of the day for the company, with no holds barred toward squeezing every dollar out of every store. Working in the restaurants had become so stressful that seasoned managers were quitting to escape the pressure. Employees demanded higher wages because the restaurants had turned into sweat shops. There was constant pressure to deliver the product at such a fast pace that the store was in an endless race against the clock.

The company's demands for optimum customer service no longer had any connection to the concept of McDonald's as an authentically customer-oriented, family-friendly environment. Customer service became a euphemism for unrelenting increases in sales and profit, once again with an eye toward Wall Street and stock prices.

That was the desperate agenda behind every new initiative. Like "couch diving" for loose change, the idea was to squeeze every dollar out of every square foot of store space and keep it up for as long as possible. First, it was extended hours for every restaurant, and then staying open twenty-four hours a day. Breakfast all day was a move in the same direction.

Yes, sales revenues will increase when a store stays open during hours when it used to be closed. Yes, stock prices may react positively to those numbers, however small the increase might be. But what needs attention is the continual added pressure on the store owners and employees who are at the bottom of the ladder. Meanwhile, profit sharing bonuses are the rewards for top management. Those in the fields reaping the crop for the company are expected to go along to get along. Don't question the masters, who know what is best for you.

Insensitivity to the many dedicated franchisees who have represented McDonald's around the world has fallen to an all-time low. A few years ago, a long-time franchisee in Houston was leaving his store to take a deposit to the bank. He was shot and killed in the parking lot of his restaurant. On behalf of his wife and family, a close friend who was also a franchisee called the president of McDonald's to inquire why, in such a tragic situation, no one had received a call of condolence from the company. The response from the then-president was both startling and revealing: "Franchisees die every day. I can't call every family when someone dies."

If I sound angry about this, it's because I am angry. But anger is not all I am. At the end of the day, we had a great career with McDonald's. We have been able to provide for our three wonderful children and put them through college. Tina and I have been married forty-four years, have worked together for thirty-five years, and have survived it all.

Everything in business has an expiration date. We reached ours with McDonald's. The shelf life of loyalty to a company can last indefinitely only if you're willing to prioritize the company over the best interests of yourself and your family. And there's no reason to feel like you've committed any sort of betrayal over that. The company knows there is always someone willing to take your place.

PART THREE

CHAPTER 21

"TINA, YOU HAVE CANCER..."

But He was wounded for our transgressions, He was bruised for our iniquities; The chastisement for our peace was upon Him, and by his stripes we are healed.

—ISAIAH 53:5

During our years together, Harold and I had become one in mind and spirit. We molded our life experiences into a single well-oiled machine. We took on all comers. We entered the McDonald's environment, the largest and most recognized fast-food company in the world, as if it were meant for us. We had all the tools necessary to be successful in whatever we chose to do.

Until...

I truly believe that nothing happens in life that is not directed by God. Based on that faith, it has become clear to me that the trials I have gone through over the past eighteen years have been for a purpose.

My first diagnosis was colorectal cancer, in 1999. Yes, I said first, only the first.

I became worried that there might be something wrong with me shortly after my father's death. He passed only two months after his diagnosis of renal cell carcinoma. I scheduled a sigmoidoscopy, which was six months after my previous colonoscopy. I then had a biopsy and was diagnosed with colorectal cancer.

When I first heard the words "Tina, you have cancer," I knew my life would be changed forever. I didn't know how it would change, I only knew this would be a life-altering experience. At that time Jeremy was twenty-one and away at college. The twins were eleven and in the fifth grade. I didn't want to share with them that I had cancer because of my father's death just six months earlier. I didn't want them to think I was going to die.

I went through chemotherapy and radiation treatments. The following June—almost a year to the date of my first diagnosis—I felt a lump in my breast. I told Harold what I felt, and he replied that it was probably nothing. I knew he was hoping that was the case, and I also knew that he probably didn't know what else to say.

I thank God I followed my intuition. No one knows your body better than you do. That is an important lesson to take from something like this. I made an appointment with my doctor and she referred me to a breast specialist.

The results of a biopsy came back positive. For the second time I was told, "Tina, you have cancer." Our kids were a year older and this time I would have to explain what I would be going through. My appearance would change, and I would not be the energetic mom they were used to.

Harold and I agreed that we would have to put up a strong front. The kids would respond to our example, and they had only us to keep them positive. I went to their elementary school graduation right after my diagnosis and sat there wondering if I would see them graduate from high school.

In order to make the right decisions, I immediately began educating myself about my diagnosis: stage two, triple negative breast cancer. There was a history of breast cancer in my family. It all sounded scary, and fear was exactly what I felt.

As I learned about my disease, my perspective did improve. I began to understand that breast cancer is not a death sentence. With a positive attitude and a belief in a healing God, I knew I would survive. I started to look at this as another season in my life.

Our business was doing well but going in everyday was no longer possible. I had to train someone to do payroll and my other responsibilities. Cleaning out my desk at the office was a depressing moment, but I knew that this was the only choice for me and the family.

I had always been a solution-oriented person. I took pride in being resilient enough to handle whatever life dealt me. But now it was hard to accept the fact that I wasn't in control of many things. What I could control was my faith in God.

I also had a loving family and a husband who would be with me all the way. I knew the memory was on his mind of how helpless he felt when his mother was dying of breast cancer. At that time, I knew I had to be a source of strength, and now I had to ask him to give strength to me.

Along with continuing to run the business and making sure that our children's lives would continue normally, we needed to have a plan and to work the plan. Harold and I talked about this and I had only one request for him during this journey.

He asked, "What can I do?"

I told him, "Your job is to make me laugh every day."

As I started my chemotherapy, every step was frightening. A port was placed in my arm, and when the drug stated to flow, I thought about the poison that was entering my body. The taste in my mouth and every smell in the room comes back to me as I write this.

The sessions would leave me tired for days. There was a cycle of fatigue following the treatments and then a gradual return of energy just before the next one. Soon my hair would start to thin and come out. I had already gone to have a wig custom made. When my hair started to fall out in clumps, Harold tried to make me laugh by playing a beautician who had done a bad job and made my hair fall out.

That provided some relief, but seeing my hair fall out was still traumatic and frightening. The wigmaker had done such a good job of matching my hair's color and style that people complimented me, assuming it was my real hair. I only took the wig off at home when I went to bed. I didn't want the kids to see me differently than they were used to.

I had a great support system, with my girlfriends taking turns going with me to have my treatments. I didn't want Harold to go because I knew it would be a difficult thing for him to watch. Every day I could see in his eyes the fear of what had happened to his mother.

I got to the other side of the chemo treatments. My hair came back, although it looked thinner than it had been. Or maybe, since I'd always had thick hair, the change was only noticeable to me. Overall, it took a long time for me to start regaining my strength.

As that was finally beginning to happen, I noticed something unusual around the site of the lumpectomy. This led to another biopsy performed in the area of the earlier one.

Once you've had a cancer diagnosis, any ache or pain or simple change in your body scares you to death. You think that everything is another cancer. The worst part is, sometimes it really is cancer. That's what I heard from my doctor when the results of the new biopsy came back positive. For the third time, "Tina, you have cancer."

My faith teaches that God will not give you more than you can bear. I have always been strong, but this was testing me beyond

Tina at the Susan G. Koman Race for the Cure in Washington, DC

belief. I didn't know if I could do this again. I was scared. By now I had met and talked with many breast cancer patients. Incredible as it seemed, many of their husbands had left them when they were diagnosed, or soon after.

I never had any concerns like that with Harold. Difficult as it was, he and I were going to relive this again. We had a bond, a love, and a commitment to each other through the vows we took. That never wavered during all the challenges we had come through, and it was not going to break us now.

This cancer fortunately was a squamous cell carcinoma, caused by the earlier radiation treatment. Only the removal of the small spot was required.

Since then, God has blessed me to be cancer free for nineteen years. I have become an activist for breast cancer screening, and I've joined the board of the Susan G. Komen Cancer Foundation and I've became a mentor and a speaker on the importance of self-examination and early detection. My daughter, Jennifer, now has a legacy of breast cancer through both grandmothers and her mother. In a very personal way I am determined to do whatever I can to eliminate this disease. I desperately want a cure to be found in my lifetime.

Harold and I always made sure that we took family vacations while the kids were young, to share as many moments together as we could. Our favorite destination was the Bahamas. When Harold was the chair of the Trumpet Awards Foundation we were able to meet the prime minister of the Bahamas, the Honorable Perry Christie. On one of our later visits, we had the opportunity to dine with the prime minister and came to know many Bahamians.

Coincidentally, the board of the Susan G. Komen Foundation had commissioned a study on the high rate of breast cancer among young Bahamian women. The study showed that the small gene pool in the islands led to a rate of diagnosis and early death higher than anywhere else in the world.

I met with the staff of Princess Margaret Hospital, which was overseeing the cancer treatments in the Bahamas. When I toured the hospital and entered the wing where women received chemotherapy, I felt as though I were having the treatments all over again. The sights, sounds, and smells were all there. A major challenge for both the hospital and the patients was providing the ports necessary for delivery of the drugs. The ports were twenty-five dollars each, which could be a financial strain in the Bahamas. And when I saw the hospital's mammography machine, it looked like something out of the Dark Ages. The staff admitted that it was difficult even to get a full image from the machine.

When I finished the hospital tour, I wrote a check for ten thousand dollars to provide ports for chemo treatments. When I returned home, I contacted the Susan G. Komen organization, and we arranged for the manufacturer of the mammography machine to donate two units to the Princess Margaret Hospital. I also established the first annual "Race for the Cure." Harold and I attended the first three years of the race.

As a cancer survivor, I remind women at every opportunity that "cancer" starts with C. You CAN get it and you CAN survive it. There is a saying that states, "You find your purpose in life when your talents meet the needs of others." This is my purpose. To fulfill it, God took me through the valley and brought me out on the other side.

CHAPTER 22

HEART AND SOUL

We go down the wrong road, we get lost, we turn back.
Maybe it doesn't matter which road we embark on.
Maybe what matters is that we embark.

—BARBARA HALL

Things happen for a reason. I deeply believe that. But what is the reason? It's there, and we have to see it.

We were scheduled to go to Hawaii for a McDonald's conference. The night before we were to leave, our dog was taken by coyotes that were in the canyon behind out house. We looked all over the neighborhood but couldn't find her. We were both devastated.

Our kids were due to come home from school the following week, on the day before we returned. Tina didn't want to go to the conference and have them come home and not find their dog. They had gotten the dog when they were small and had grown up with it. I couldn't convince Tina to go, and I decided that I wouldn't go either.

About two in the morning I woke up and found Tina sitting on the side of the bed. I asked her why she was awake, and she told me

176

that she had indigestion. When she was still feeling uncomfortable an hour later, I asked if we should call our doctor, who happened to live across the street from us. She said no, but she had been on the computer looking at symptoms of a heart attack in women.

I was not okay with her refusal and told her to call Charles across the street. He was a chief of cardiology at Sharp Hospital in San Diego. Tina called him and described what was going on. He asked a few questions and said that it was better to be safe than sorry. He would meet her at the hospital.

When we arrived at the hospital, an admitting nurse met us at the door. She said Charles was waiting in the emergency room. As sometimes happens when a patient is about to see a doctor, Tina said she was suddenly feeling much better. As she was talking with Jeremy, who by that time had arrived at the hospital, Charles said he wanted to do an EKG.

After the test, Tina and I were talking when Charles came in the room. Tina said, "Can I go home?"

Charles gave her a slight smile and said, "I don't think so. You're having a heart attack."

One of the medications Tina was given with her chemotherapy was known to affect arteries in the heart. She was stunned because she generally felt fine, other than needing to burp.

Charles walked with Tina to the operating room. Tina didn't notice that Charles had put a chase cart machine on the gurney in case her heart failed on the way. A stent was placed in a main artery, which was found to be 90 percent blocked. The artery is called "the widow maker." Tim Russet, the news anchor, died of a blockage in that artery.

Charles had called in a surgeon who was a specialist in stents and the procedure was completed in thirty minutes. Charles showed me some frightening images of the artery before and after the stent. He also told me that if we had gotten on the plane to Hawaii and the artery closed, she would had not have made it.

We understood this to mean that our dog had somehow been Tina's saving angel. It was not Tina's time yet. Her journey wasn't finished. There was still work for her to do then, and there is still work for her to do now. What's more, there is still work for us to do together.

In San Diego, when we had grown to eight restaurants and our work around the city was well known, I was appointed to the Qualcomm Stadium Advisory Board by the mayor of San Diego. The board oversaw the operations of the stadium where the San Diego Chargers played.

When I arrived at the stadium for my first board meeting, I had learned from experience not to be surprised that I was the only African American on the ten-member board. I took my seat and was reading the agenda for the meeting when an elderly man sitting across from me said, "You must be Harold Lewis. You own a bunch of McDonald's restaurants, don't you?"

Before I could respond, he continued, "Do they have special program for you people?"

I paused a beat to contemplate my answer, then took a deep breath and said, "Yes, they require hard work and money."

So it was happening again. It was happening as it had when the Ferrari had been delivered and when my mother had bought the Flagstone Hotel for Sister McLaney. What had I learned since then? I had learned to distinguish between a racist and an old man who didn't even realize that what he'd said was insulting.

The city provided the board members with a private box at the stadium for all the events that were held there, not just the football games. The old man turned out to be a great guy. He was always nice to my kids and to anyone who came to the box with me. He was very liberal and would have been hurt if I had gotten angry at his question. I was glad I didn't respond the way that I would have in my younger days.

But while his attitude was progressive, his behavior had not caught up with his principles. I hope that mine has, or someday will.

CHAPTER 23

WHAT MATTERS MOST

Life does not come with an instruction manual,
but it will make you out of a story.
Life is more than a fairytale.

—NYA LEE

M y early life in Louisiana was family, church, and school. It was within a framework of the segregated South and the Creole community in that restricted environment. The Creole community had a sense of itself as a village. Everyone had to look out for each other. If there was need on someone's part, a way had to be found to fill the need. For instance, the community needed schools. My family was in the construction business and had practical skills to meet that need. They built the parish school that my siblings and I attended.

Harold's experiences growing up in Los Angeles were like night and day compared to the segregation I experienced in the South. Harold never saw a sign reading "White Only" or "Colored Only." His life experiences gave him role models to look up to and helped frame his view of the world from an entirely different perspective.

Tina's home in Baton Rouge, Louisiana, built by her father in 1947 at age nineteen

He was able to envision himself in places that I had never imagined, and to see people who looked like him in positions of power and dignity. His life ceiling was limitless compared to mine.

Harold's exposure and surroundings in Los Angeles allowed him to have opportunities that few Black men experience. The foundation of his father and family running a business had programed him to be a leader and not a follower. For that reason, as he began his career, he never felt out of place or that he didn't belong. He did understand the challenges he would face, but he had been given the inner strength to navigate the minefields of the subtle discrimination that did exist. That was something very different from overt Southern racism.

But Harold would suffer the loss of his father at age seven, while nothing like that happened to me. Maybe we arrived at some of the same feelings by different paths.

I grew up next door to my paternal grandparents. The family hierarchy in the South was patrilocal, unlike the matriarchal family that Harold grew up in. I was one of eleven children, playing dodgeball in the backyard with my siblings and my cousins, and my grandmother had to take charge. There were no public playgrounds for us in the segregated South.

As much as they could, my family sheltered me from the racial bias that surrounded us. For the first twelve years of my life, I lived in a bubble—but the dolls I played with were White and everything I saw on television or in movies was about White people. Will it be that way again, or has it ever really changed? Today when I see news of police violence against Black people and racial profiling, I feel that I'm seeing the past rise up like the lost city of Atlantis.

The hard work that Harold and I did for so many years in airlines, print shops, and restaurants seemed so important at the time. And it was important. After thirty years in McDonald's, we felt we had put down a good foundation for our kids to build upon. We had been recognized both inside and outside of the company for our accomplishments. Jeremy had become a franchisee and Jonathan and Jennifer were in the program to become franchisees as well. Our story had been documented by Black History Makers and is housed in the Library of Congress for perpetuity.

But when I look back at it now and try to decide what I'm most proud of, work and business are not what come to mind. I'm glad that I've been married for forty-four years and that we have three wonderful children. I'm glad that I'm a three-time cancer survivor and that I've been able to help others survive. Onward. Life is sometimes like driving down the highway. You can sometimes get into mental cruise control and not really pay attention to where you're going. But if you don't pay attention, you can miss your blessing.

We have been on a journey through many twists and turns, and when we have thought all was lost in the midnight hour, God has turned it around in our favor again and again.

> *And we know that all things work together for good to*
> *those who love God, and to those who are the called*
> *according to His purpose.*
>
> —ROMANS 8:28

Acknowledgments

For their insight and inspiration, we are deeply grateful to Nena Oshman, Austin Miller, Sandy Aston, Bishop Clinton House, Roland Martin, Stedman Graham, and Hon. Ambassador Andrew Young. Many thanks also to Mitch Sisskind and Debra Englander for their help in preparing the manuscript for publication.

About the Authors

Harold and Tina Lewis formed the HRL Group and together built and operated twenty McDonald's restaurants over the past thirty years. The Lewis family relocated from San Diego, California to Las Vegas where they retired after selling their restaurants. They possess a wealth of knowledge and expertise in the field of business management.

Married for forty-four years and business partners for thirty-five years, Harold and Tina have managed to successfully organize and administer their business while raising three children. Jeremy, age forty, was a successful second-generation franchisee, and Jonathan and Jennifer are thirty-year-old twins.

Since opening their first restaurant, the Lewises have contributed numerous hours and resources to a variety of McDonald's programs, community organizations, and causes. The McDonald's corporation has recognized them with some of the highest honors for excellence in community service, including the prestigious "Ronald Award" and McDonald's outstanding store award, one of the company's highest recognitions for excellence in store operation.

The Lewis' also founded the AVAIL (African American Visionary and Inspirational Leaders) scholarship program which to date has awarded more $850,000 to help students to pursue a college education. They have additionally given scholarships through the Trumpet

Awards Foundation. In 2011 the Lewis Family Foundation established the UNLV/Jennifer Lewis Scholarship fund, and formed the mountain Top Faith Ministries scholarship fund for graduating high school students.

In addition, Harold served as the Chairman of the Trumpet Awards Foundation. Tina served on the National speakers Bureau and board for the Susan G. Komen for the cure foundation. They have been the recipients of many awards, including The Jackie Robinson YMCA, Dr. Martin Luther King Jr. Human Dignity Award, UNCF Frederick D. Patterson Award, The California Legislature Assembly Entrepreneurial Spirit Award, Urban League Equal Opportunity Award, and the KPBS Living Legend Award, among others.

Their oral and video history has been made a permanent part of the History Makers collection at the Library of Congress.